Luther's Liturgical Criteria and his Reform of The Canon of The Mass

Bryan Spinks
Churchill College, Cambridge

GROVE BOOKS

BRAMCOTE   NOTTS.

CONTENTS

Copyright Bryan Spinks 1982

PREFACE

Among the many reasons for which the name Luther is remembered and venerated, that of 'liturgiologist' rarely figures in the English-speaking world. As a liturgiologist, the Wittenberg Reformer has gone unnoticed, and the common opinion seems to be that his endeavours in this field were ultra-conservative and unnecessarily clumsy and destructive. This study seeks to question this widespread opinion, and attempts to let Luther answer for himself. A concluding section sketches some of the questions Luther poses for the composition of eucharistic prayers today.

I would like to record my sincere thanks to the Rev. Ronald Feuerhahn, Praeceptor of Westfield House, Cambridge, who kindly put at my disposal the library of Westfield House; has allowed me to quote from his M.Phil. Thesis on Luther's liturgical reforms; and kindly read through the draft of this study and offered suggestions from a Lutheran point of view.

I am also grateful to the Rev. Dr. George Newlands of the Divinity School, Cambridge, who also read through the text, and offered encouraging (and amusing), suggestions.

The cover picture of Luther is the portrait by Lukas Cranach, dated 1525/6, which is in the Kunstmuseum, Basel, and is reproduced with kind permission.

Abbreviations
LW   American edition of *Luther's Works,* (Philadelphia and St. Louis, 1955—) (American spelling has been retained).
WA   D. Martin *Luthers Werke,* (Weimar, 1883—)
LR   *Liturgical Review*
OCA   Orientalia Christinana Analecta
SL   *Studia Liturgica*

First Impression June 1982

ISSN 0306 0608
ISBN 0 907536 24 7

1. LUTHER MISJUDGED?

Luther's Liturgical Work

Although Martin Luther is readily acknowledged as the catalyst and leader of the Reformation in Germany, and as an outstanding exegete and preacher, amongst English-speaking students of liturgy his name is not as readily associated with liturgical reform in the same way as, for example, are the names of Thomas Cranmer or Martin Bucer. Nevertheless, finding himself as helmsman of the German Reformation movement, Luther was called upon to offer guidelines for liturgical revision, and these guidelines became determinative for the whole subsequent history and development of Lutheran worship. Perhaps the best known of Luther's reforms are the *Formula Missae* of 1523 (*FM*) and his *Deutsche Messe* of 1526 (*DM*); but he also produced two baptismal rites (1523 and 1526), an Order of Marriage (1529), an Order for Confession, a German and Latin Litany (1529), and an Ordination rite.[1] He also offered guides and suggestions for the Divine Office, and for the general ordering of worship, and he composed collects, canticles, and hymns, as well as producing music. While in comparison with the rest of his literary output, Luther's liturgical work may seem insignificant, it amounts to no less than that of other Reformation liturgical reformers, and its influence has been considerable.

The main concern of this study is Luther's liturgical criteria and the rationale of his reform of the canon of the mass as represented by *FM* and *DM*. At the outset, therefore, it is necessary to have before us Luther's suggestions for the reform of that part of the mass.

(1) From the *Formula Missae* 1523:[1]

> II *The bread and wine having been prepared, one may proceed as follows:*
>> The Lord be with you.
>> *Response:* **And with thy spirit.**
>> Lift up your hearts.
>> *Response:* **Let us lift them to the Lord.**
>> Let us give thanks unto the Lord our God.
>> *Response:* **It is meet and right.**
>> It is truly meet and right, just and salutary for us to give thanks to thee always and everywhere, Holy Lord, Father Almighty, Eternal God, through Christ our Lord . . .
>
> III *Then:*
>> . . . Who the day before he suffered, took bread, and when he had given thanks, brake it, and gave it to his disciples, saying, Take, eat; this is my body, which is given for you.

---

[1] *LW* 53: Bryan D. Spinks, 'Luther's Taufbüchlein 1 in *LR* 5:2 (1975), pp.17-20; 'Luther's Taufbüchlein 2, in *LR* 6:1 (1976), pp.13-21; 'Luther's Other Major Liturgical Reforms; 1. The Divine Office, and the German and "Latin Litany Corrected" ' in *LR* 7:1 (1977), pp.35-44: 'Luther's Other Major Liturgical Reforms: 2. The Ordination of Ministers of the Word' in *LR* 9:1 (1979), pp.20-32; 'Luther's Other Major Liturgical Reforms: 3. The Taufbüchlein' in *LR* 10:1 (1980), pp.33-38.

[2] *LW* 53.27-29.

After the same manner also the cup, when he had supped, saying, This cup is the New Testament in my blood, which is shed for you and for many, for the remission of sins; this do, as often as ye do it, in remembrance of me.

I wish these words of Christ—with a brief pause after the preface—to be recited in the same tone in which the Lord's Prayer is chanted elsewhere in the canon so that those who are present may be able to hear them, although the evangelically minded should be free about all these things and may recite these words either silently or audibly.

IV. *The blessing ended, let the choir sing the Sanctus. And while the Benedictus is being sung, let the bread and cup be elevated according to the customary rite for the benefit of the weak in faith who might be offended if such an obvious change in this rite of the mass were suddenly made. This concession can be made especially where through sermons in the vernacular they have been taught what the elevation means.*

Showing God to his people

V. *After this, the Lord's Prayer shall be read. Thus,* Let us pray: 'Taught by thy saving precepts . . .' *The prayer which follows,* 'Deliver us, we beseech thee . . .,' *is to be omitted together with all the signs they were accustomed to make over the host and with the host over chalice. Nor shall the host be broken or mixed into the chalice. But immediately after the Lord's Prayer shall be said,* 'The peace of the Lord,' *etc., which is, so to speak, a public absolution of the sins of the communicants, the true voice of the gospel announcing remission of sins, and therefore the one and most worthy preparation for the Lord's Table, if faith holds to these words as coming from the mouth of Christ himself. On this account I would like to have it pronounced facing the people, as the bishops are accustomed to do, which is the only custom of the ancient bishops that is left among our bishops.*

VI. *Then, while the Agnus Dei is sung, let him (the minister) communicate, first himself and then the people. But if he should wish to pray the prayer.* 'O Lord Jesus Christ, Son of the living God, who according to the will of the Father,' *etc., before communicating, he does not pray wrongly, provided he changes the singular* 'mine' *and* 'me' *to the plural* 'ours' *and* 'us'. *The same thing holds for the prayer,* 'The body of our Lord Jesus Christ preserve my (or thy) soul unto life eternal,' *and,* 'The blood of our Lord preserve thy soul unto life eternal'.

It should be noted that the *Formula Missae* was a Latin mass.

(2) From the *Deutsche Messe* 1526:[1]

After the sermon shall follow a public paraphrase of the Lord's Prayer and admonition for those who want to partake of the sacrament, in this or a better fashion:

Friends in Christ: Since we are here assembled in the name of the Lord to receive his Holy Testament, I admonish you first of all to lift up your hearts to God to pray with me the Lord's Prayer, as Christ our Lord has taught us and graciously promised to hear us.

That God, our Father in heaven, may look with mercy on us, his needy children on earth, and grant us grace so that his holy name be hallowed by us all the world through the pure and true teaching of his Word and the fervent love of our lives; that he would graciously turn from us all false doctrine and evil living whereby his precious name is being blasphemed and profaned.

That his kingdom may come to us and expand; that all transgressors and they who are blinded and bound in the devil's kingdom be brought to know Jesus Christ his Son by faith, and that the number of Christians may be increased.

That we may be strengthened by his Spirit to do and to suffer his will, both in life and in death, in good and in evil things, and always to break, slay and sacrifice our own wills.

That he would also give us our daily bread, preserve us from greed and selfish cares, and help us to trust that he will provide for all our needs.

That he would forgive our debts as we forgive our debtors so that our hearts may rest and rejoice in a good conscience before him, and that no sin may ever fright or alarm us.

That he would not lead us into temptation but help us by his Spirit to subdue the flesh, to depise the world and its ways, and to overcome the devil with all his wiles.

And lastly, that he would deliver us from all evil, both of body and soul, now and forever.

All those who earnestly desire these things will say from their very hearts: Amen, trusting without any doubt that it is Yea and answered in heaven as Christ has promised: Whatever you ask in prayer, believe that you shall receive it, and you will [Mark 11.24]. Amen.

Secondly, I admonish you in Christ that you discern the Testament of Christ in true faith and, above all, take to heart the words wherein Christ imparts to us his body and his

[1] *LW* 53.78-82.

blood for the remission of our sins. That you remember and give thanks for his boundless love which he proved to us when he redeemed us from God's wrath, sin, death, and hell by his own blood. And that in this faith you externally receive the bread and wine, i.e., his body and his blood, as the pledge and guarantee of this. In his name therefore, and according to the command that he gave, let us use and receive the Testament.

Whether such paraphrase and admonition should be read in the pulpit immediately after the sermon or at the altar, I would leave to everyone's judgment. It seems that the ancients did so in the pulpit, so that it is still the custom to read general prayers or to repeat the Lord's Prayer in the pulpit. But the admonition itself has since become a public confession. In this way, however, the Lord's Prayer together with a short exposition would be current among the people, and the Lord would be remembered, even as he commanded at the Supper.

I would, however, like to ask that this paraphrase or admonition follow a prescribed wording or be formulated in a definite manner for the sake of the common people. We cannot have one do it one way today, and another, another way tomorrow, and let everybody parade his talents and confuse the people so that they can neither learn nor retain anything. What chiefly matters is the teaching and guiding of the people. That is why here we must limit our freedom and keep to one form of paraphrase or admonition, particularly in a given church or congregation—if for the sake of freedom it does not wish to use another.

Thereupon the Office and Consecration to the following tune:

It seems to me that it would accord with [the institution of] the Lord's Supper to administer the sacrament immediately after the

consecration of the bread, before the cup is blessed; for both Luke and Paul say: He took the cup after they had supped, etc. (Luke 22.20;1 Cor. 11.25). Meanwhile, the German Sanctus or the hymn, 'Let God be Blest', or the hymn of John Huss, 'Jesus Christ, Our God and Saviour', could be sung. Then shall the cup be blessed and administered, while the remainder of these hymns are sung, or the German Agnus Dei. Let there be a decent and orderly approach, not men and women together, but the women after the men, wherefore they should also stand apart from each other in separate places. What should be done about private confession, I have written elsewhere, and my opinion can be found in the 'Betbüchlein'.

We do not want to abolish the elevation, but retain it because it goes well with the German Sanctus and signifies that Christ has commanded us to remember him. For just as the sacrament is bodily elevated, and yet Christ's body and blood are not seen in it, so he is also remembered and elevated by the word of the sermon and is confessed and adored in the reception of the sacrament. In each case he is apprehended only by faith; for we cannot see how Christ gives his body and blood for us and even now daily shows and offers it before God to obtain grace for us.

The German Sanctus

I - sa - iah 'twas the proph - et who did see
Seat - ed a - bove the Lord in maj - es - ty High on a
loft - y throne in splen-dor bright; The train of his robe filled
the tem-ple quite. Stand-ing be - side him were two ser - a - phim;
Six wings, six wings he saw on each of them. With twain they hid
in awe their fac - es clear; With twain they hid their feet in rev-

'rent fear. And with the oth - er twain they flew a - bout:
One to the oth - er loud - ly raised the shout: Ho - ly is God,
the Lord of Sab - a - oth, Ho - ly is God, the Lord of Sab -
a - oth, Ho - ly is God, the Lord of Sab - a - oth, Be - hold
his glo - ry fill - eth all the earth. The an - gels' cry made beams
and lin - tels shake; The house al - so was filled with clouds of smoke.

Luther according to some English and American Liturgical Textbooks

The English-speaking student who enquires into the liturgical work of Luther will soon discover that in the general textbooks on liturgical history there is a consensus of opinion that in this particular field, the Wittenberg Reformer was conservative, hasty, and singularly inept, and that when he came to reform the canon, his method was one of drastic curtailment, amputation, and displacement.

We may begin with *An Outline of Christian Worship* by W. D. Maxwell.[1] Maxwell describes Luther as the most conservative of all Reformers in his theory of worship, but in practice he made drastic and far-reaching changes.[2] According to Maxwell, Luther was concerned that worship should be intelligible, and as a result his services were didactic. Regarding the mass, there is a sharp contradiction between his insistence on the Real Presence and his repudiation of sacrifice and offertory. Commenting on Luther's reform of the canon in *FM,* he asserts:

'. . . his treatment of the Canon is negative, illogical, and subversive. By an indefensible innovation he attaches the Words of Institution to the Preface, then adds the *Sanctus* and *Benedictus qui venit;* these latter are sung by the choir, and during the *Benedictus qui venit* the elevation takes place. The remainder of the Canon is omitted, so the rite contains neither intercessions nor a consecration prayer.'[3]

Maxwell can describe the whole reform of the canon as 'unconstructive and negative'.[4] Regarding *DM,* Maxwell writes:

'He deals drastically with the Liturgy of the Faithful, sadly mutilating it beyond what the Lutheran teaching required, and providing a most inadequate vehicle of devotion. . . . The whole of the Canon except the Words of Institution is abolished; and the rite contains no prayer of consecration, thanksgiving, or intercession. The elevation is retained, and consecration is affected by reading the Words of Institution over the elements.'[5]

In his concluding remarks, Maxwell asserts that although *DM* gave the people a more intelligible part to play, as a form it was defective, and Luther's own positive contribution to worship is to be seen in hymnody. In his opinion, the Swedish and Norwegian Lutheran rites were more creative.

The views of W. D. Maxwell, a liturgist of the Reformed tradition, were quoted with approval by another writer of the same tradition, Raymond Abba, in *Principles of Christian Worship.*[6] But the denomination or tradition seems of little significance. The Anglican liturgical scholar, G. J. Cuming, writes in a similar vein. Having described the order of *FM* where Luther 'sweeps' away references to offertory, and the canon is 'reduced' to the words of institution, he writes:

'These conservative alterations were only a first step, and in 1526, Luther issued a drastic revision of each service.'[7]

[1] W. D. Maxwell *An Outline of Christian Worship* (Oxford, 1936).

[2] *Ibid.,* p.73.

[3] *Ibid.,* p.77. Maxwell, it should be noted, seems to take *Apostolic Constitutions* 8 as a model by which other rites may be judged.

[4] *Ibid.,* p.78.

[5] *Ibid.,* p.79.

[6] Raymond Abba *Principles of Christian Worship* (Oxford, 1959), Maxwell was a minister of the Church of Scotland, and Abba a Congregationalist.

[7] G. J. Cuming *A History of Anglican Liturgy* (MacMillan, First edition, London, 1969) pp.33, 34.

And reflecting on *DM,*
> 'Luther's ideas were hastily conceived and sometimes contra-
> dictory. . . . His fear of retaining any traces of the medieval
> doctrine of sacrifice led him into an excessively violent treatment
> of the Canon; but his sense of the numinous element in the Mass
> enabled him to preserve some of the medieval devotional feeling.
> The great importance which he attached to the concept of
> fellowship ensured the continuance of the weekly celebration of
> the Lord's Supper as the central feature of Lutheran worship.'[1]

In the recent study written to 'produce an introduction to the study of
liturgy for students in all our churches throughout the English-speaking
world', although it is acknowledged that Luther's work is more than a
simplification of the Latin mass, and his theology has the decisive
word, the Reformer's eucharistic revisions are linked with the word
'conservative', and the canon with 'excision' and 'cut out'.[2] Likewise
Geoffrey Wainwright asserts that Luther's method of reforming the
canon was to 'excise' the sacrificial prayers, and in both *FM* and *DM,*
the words of institution alone remain[3]; 'a hatchet job' is the description
offered by Donald Bridge and David Phypers.[4]

This same assessment of Luther reappears in some influential
American liturgical works.

Students of the Lutheran tradition owe a great debt to Dr. Luther D.
Reed's book, *The Lutheran Liturgy.*[5] Dr. Reed's concern was to put the
Common Service Book of the United Lutheran Church, USA, in context,
and to explain and commend this liturgy. He was also concerned to
explain and justify the fact that modern Lutheran Churches are adopting
a eucharistic prayer modelled upon the classical anaphoras. Drawing
upon many Continental and American scholars, Reed describes
Luther's liturgical work in the context of the history of liturgy.

Reed explains that, to begin with, Luther never sought to abolish the
historic order and substitute a new service, for he reverenced the forms
which faith had built, and recognized that the whole devotional and
ceremonial system of the church was deeply impressed upon popular
imagination.[6] Luther's *FM* was conservative, but its conservatism is not
that of timidity, but of courageous conviction. Furthermore, there was a
pedagogical purpose:
> 'The first thought is to express faith; the final purpose is, perhaps
> too restrictedly, to create more faith.'[7]

[1] *Ibid.,* p.35.
[2] C. Jones, G. Wainwright, E. Yarnold, (eds.) *The Study of Liturgy* (S.P.C.K., London, 1978) p.xviii; pp.252, 437.
[3] G. Wainwright *Doxology. The Praise of God in Worship, Doctrine and Life.* (Epworth, London, 1980) pp.269, 329.
[4] Donald Bridge and David Phypers *The Meal that Unites* (Hodder and Stoughton, London, 1981)). p.92.
[5] L. D. Reed *The Luteran Liturgy* (Fortress, Philadelphia, 1947; Revised edition, 1959). The references are to the Revised edition.
[6] *Ibid.,* pp.69-70.
[7] *Ibid.,* p.74.

Luther's most radical reform of the liturgy was the omission of the offertory and canon.[1] His *FM* cut out everything in the canon except the Verba, which the minister was ordered to chant aloud; in *DM* he placed a paraphrase of the Lord's Prayer first, and followed this by the Verba.[2] His action was rather like a surgeon at work.[3] Regarding Luther's treatment of the Sanctus in *FM* Reed writes:

'Unquestionably this unhistorical arrangement loses the original force of the Sanctus as a natural and beautiful climax to the Preface, disorganizes the historic framework of the liturgy to reinforce a particular doctrine, and breaks with the order of other Luteran churches and with that of the church universal to establish a provincial use.'[4]

And in *DM*:

'Luther in his German Mass (1526) with a sense of hymnological rather than of liturgical values, paraphrased the Sanctus in the form of a German hymn, to be sung by the congregation during the distribution. Unfortunately, in point of literary and poetic values, this was the least happy of Luther's liturgical and hymnological endeavours. Apart from that, it gives only the story of Isaiah 6.1 and does not include the praise of the congregation.'[5]

However, the reason why the Sanctus was placed after the Verba may reflect a medieval custom of singing the Sanctus and Benedictus during the consecration and elevation.[6]

According to Reed, Luther could be charged with inconsistency. In his reform of the canon, the Verba were left isolated; the 'operation' left a gaping void. Reed also notes that the Luteran tradition on the whole did not approve the suggestions of the *DM* of substituting an exhortation for the Preface, division of the Verba, and retention of the elevation.[7] In his opinion, *FM* was Luther's greatest liturgical writing, and in the field of *music,* his work was creative and pioneering.[8]

According to the Roman Catholic scholar Louis Bouyer, in his important book *Eucharist* (ET, Notre Dame, Indiana), Luther's determination to get rid of the notion of Christ's sacrifice in the mass resulted in the removal from the canon of everything which expressed such a notion. Yet, in doing so, he merely stretched the logic of the medieval Latin idea that only the words of institution, isolated from their traditional context, were essential for the eucharistic consecration. In Bouyer's opinion, the form of the canon in *FM* and *DM* represents:

'. . . an ultimate deformation of that type which reduced everything to the adoration of the real presence, consecrated solely by the Words of Institution, before a communion in which forgiveness of sins absorbs all other aspects of the believers union with the crucified Savior.'[9]

---

[1] *Ibid.,* p.334.　　[4] *Ibid.,* p.332.　　[7] *Ibid.,* p.78.
[2] *Ibid.,* p.340.　　[5] *Ibid.,*　　　　　　 [8] *Ibid.,* pp.72, 86.
[3] *Ibid.,* p.346.　　[6] cf. p.343.
[9] L. Bouyer *Eucharist* (ET. E. Quinn, Notre Dame, Indiana, 1968) p.388. cf. pp.385-6.

Bard Thomson refers to Luther's conservatism, and suggests that he assaulted the canon with pure Thuringian invective.[1] James F. White suggests that Luther is conservative until he comes to the canon, 'which he slashes down to the words of institution and sanctus'.[2] Eugene Brand, an influential American Lutheran liturgist, has offered a critique of Luther's work on the eucharist under the title 'Luther's liturgical surgery'[3]; and another Lutheran, Frank C. Senn, in an article on *FM* states that Luther did not discard the canon but drastically revised it, limiting it to the Preface, the Sanctus and the institution narrative, displacing the sanctus from its historical position by attaching the narrative of institution to the Preface.[4]

In the face of such a formidable consensus, it might seem that any dissent from this estimate of Luther's work must be highly questionable. However, a careful examination of the footnotes and bibliographies of these works reveals an interesting fact. All make use of, or cite as authoritative, a single work by the Swedish Lutheran scholar, Bishop Yngve Brilioth.[5] An investigation of Brilioth reveals that we are *not* dealing with the opinions and results of independent investigations by numerous scholars, but simply the constant repetition by successive scholars of the views promulgated by Brilioth. Repetition of these views do not make them assured results of liturgical scholarship! It is necessary, therefore, to look more closely at what Brilioth said.

Luther and the Canon of the Mass according to Yngve Brilioth

Brilioth's *Eucharistic Faith and Practice, Evangelical and Catholic* was published in English in 1930.[6] The original Swedish work was entitled *Nattvarden i evangeliskt gudstjantliv,* and had appeared in 1926. The book did not purport to be a history of the eucharistic liturgy in the same way as did W. D. Maxwell's *An Outline of Christian Worship.* Behind Brilioth's investigation lay the challenges to the integrity of the eucharist posed by Liberal Protestantism—David Strauss, Bruno Bauer, and Ernest Renan, together with Spitta, Harnack and Jülicher.[7] For an overall view of the literature, Brilioth appealed to Albert Schweitzer's *Das Abendmahl im Zusammenhang mit dem Leben Jesu und der*

[1] Bard Thompson *Liturgies of the Western Church* (World Publishing Company, New York, 1962) p.99.

[2] James F. White *Introduction to Christian Worship* (Abingdon, Nashville, Tennessee, 1980) p.219.

[3] E. Brand, 'Luther's Liturgical Surgery', in Fred W. Meuser and Stanley D. Schneider (eds.) *Interpreting Luther's Legacy* (Augsburg, Minneapolis, 1969) pp.108-119; also section 9, 'Lutheran' under the article 'Liturgies' in J. G. Davies (ed.) *A Dictionary of Liturgy and Worship* (S.C.M., London, 1972) pp.236-238.

[4] Frank C. Senn, 'Martin Luther's Revision of the Eucharistic Canon in the *Formula Missae* of 1523' in *Concordia Theological Monthly* 44 (1973), pp.101-118.

[5] All these sources quote Brilioth, but then the newer works quote predecessors as an added authenticity. E.g. Abba cites Maxwell and Brilioth; Cuming quotes Brilioth and Maxwell; Senn quotes Bouyer and Brilioth. Eugene Brand seems to have depended on L. D. Reed.

[6] Y. Brilioth *Eucharistic Faith and Practice, Evangelical and Catholic* (translated by A. G. Hebert, (S.P.C.K., London, 1930)).

[7] *Ibid.* pp.3-4.

Geschichte des Urchristentums (1901), which grouped the literature under two headings. The first group emphasized the memorial-aspect, the act of Jesus at the Last Supper regarded as a symbolic action setting forth the passion. This view tended regularly to the acceptance of the record of the institution as authentic, but it did not succeed in explaining how and why the act came to be repeated in the eucharist of the primitive church.[1] The second type of view laid stress on the reception of the bread and wine in the act of communion, which readily explained the repetition of the rite in the church, but regarded its association with the passion as an aetiological cult legend.[2] Schweitzer's own view, stressing the authenticity and originality of the Marcan account, and the eschatological outlook of Mark 14.25, was regarded by Brilioth as failing to explain how the rite ever came to be repeated in the primitive church. Furthermore, Lietzmann's *Messe und Herrenmahl* (1926) posited two different types of primitive eucharist; one which derived from Jewish family meals which Jesus celebrated with his disciples, and a second type which derived from St. Paul. The problem, therefore, said Brilioth, could be stated in two questions:

1. Can the eucharist of the church still be derived from the action of Jesus in the night that he was betrayed?
2. Can any particular view of the rite be established on the basis of the New Testament evidence as the norm and standard by which all subsequent developments are to be judged?[3]

Brilioth argued that an affirmative answer could be given to the first question. With regard to the second, he suggested that the New Testament evidence was rich and manifold. There were antitheses found in the rite between a glad meal of fellowship and the memorial of the Lord's Passion, and between the part of the communicants and that of the Lord. These, he suggested, comprised four main elements:

1. *Thanksgiving,* or Eucharist.
2. *Communion-fellowship.*
3. *Commemoration,* or the historical side.
4. Sacrifice, including the act of memorial, and the church's self-oblation.

To these Brilioth added a fifth: *Mystery,* which embraces and unites all the others, and bridges the gap between the one act of the Saviour and the innumerable eucharists in which that act is apprehended in the experience of faith, and its benefits appropriated.[4] (We might term this fifth element 'Presence'.).

It was from this list of categories or elements that Brilioth then proceeded to describe and evaluate the historic liturgies, from the Didache onwards, though concentrating on the Western tradition. It was a 'Motif-research' approach, with a theology of eucharistic worship in mind; it was not intended as a history of the eucharistic liturgy. In the course of his investigation, Brilioth was not only able to evaluate different rites in the terms of his motifs, but he was also able to indulge in comparative liturgy. As a Swedish Lutheran, he gave a considerable amount of space to the Swedish Lutheran rites—the chapter in the English translation was a condensation of the corresponding section of

---

[1] *Ibid.,* p.3.   [2] *Ibid.*   [3] *Ibid.,* p.2.   [4] *Ibid.,* pp.16-17.

the original Swedish work. It is within this context that we must see Brilioth's discussion of Luther's liturgical work, for although he gave a masterly and sympathetic account of Luther's eucharistic theology, Luther's rites were examined and judged not only in terms of the five elements which Brilioth regarded as a norm or standard, but also in the light of the classical rites, and the Swedish 'enriched' Lutheran rites.

According to Brilioth, Luther retained throughout his life a deep religious impression from the old Latin service, which never allowed him to lose hold of the element of Mystery in the eucharist, nor to break altogether with the traditional forms of the church's worship.[1] In his sermon *De digna praeparatione cordis pro suscipiendo sacramento eucharistiae* (1518) and in *The Blessed Sacrament of the Holy and True Body of Christ, and the Brotherhoods* (1519), he stresses fellowship and communion, but in his *Lectures on Hebrews* and the *Babylonian Captivity,* the strong element of Mystery comes out in the idea of Testament; the eucharist is a testament of forgiveness of sins. While he attacks the idea of the sacrifice of the mass in his anti-Roman writings, he upheld the real presence—and hence the mystery of the eucharist—against the 'spiritualizers' such as Zwingli. Brilioth's discussion of Luther's understanding of the eucharist was clear and lucid, and remains a valuable introduction.

However, when Brilioth turned to Luther's liturgical reforms, he began with the assertion:

'On the liturgical side the Lutheran Reformation showed little creative power; and this is especially true of Luther himself. The conservative and unpractical side of his mind comes out in the fact that he was never really interested in liturgical forms; to him they were indifferent things, wherein a man might be content to conform to the established usage.'[2]

It is regrettable that Brilioth should have prefaced his examination of Luther's eucharistic forms with such a dogmatic statement, for even if this were true of the eucharist, Brilioth offered no evidence at all that such as assessment was valid for all Luther's liturgical work. Furthermore, while it is true that Luther regarded liturgical ceremonies as indifferent things (*adiaphora*), it is a mistake to interpret this to mean that Luther himself had no interest in them.[3] Brilioth himself noted how the extreme liturgical reforms of Karlstadt, for example, alarmed Luther, and prompted him to action. Had Luther have been indifferent in the way Brilioth suggests, he would have been uninterested in the reforms of Karlstadt.

When Brilioth turned to consider *FM,* he gave a general description of Luther's suggestion for the outline of the service, noting a conservative treatment of the Liturgy of the Word. However, of eucharistic proper, and the stress on sacrifice in the medieval mass, he asserted:

'Here, therefore, the pruning-knife must be more rigorously applied; and of the latter half of the service only a torso is left.'[4]

[1] *Ibid.,* pp.95ff.
[2] *Ibid.,* p.110.
[3] On *Adiaphora,* see below, p.22.
[4] Brilioth, *op. cit.,* p.116.

Comparing *FM* directly with the canon of the mass, Brilioth explained that Luther attached the words of institution to the *'per Jesum Christum Dominum nostrum'* of the 'mutilated' preface. Commenting on the fact that the Sanctus comes after the Institution narrative, Brilioth wrote: 'The transposition of the Sanctus and the words of institution is without doubt one of the least successful of Luther's suggestions for reform. Two reasons are conceivable: either, because he was accustomed to attach the real presence to the words of institution, he felt an impropriety in singing the Benedictus qui venit at an earlier point; or it may be simply that he found this to be a simple way of making a grammatical connection with the words of institution. In a variety of ways this arrangement has kept its place in various Lutheran liturgies; and the Swedish mass still perpetuates the false step.'[1]

Brilioth was equally critical of *DM*. The Preface showed how 'unclear and contradictory his liturgical ideas still were'.[2] His overall assessment was that the 'weak points' of these reforms were the dislocation of the Preface and Sanctus, and the loss of both in *DM*. Corporate fellowship was lacking, and individual communion was emphasized to the exclusion of *koinonia;* the commemorative aspect was represented only by the words of institution, with a stress on the passion, and the sacrifice of ourselves with Christ was never given liturgical (i.e. linguistic) form. Judging Luther's reforms in the light of his five elements, Brilioth concluded that the Reformer's greatest postive merit was the introduction of German hymns and music; here 'Luther's contribution is that of genius'.[3]

It is clear—from phraseology, footnotes, and bibliography—that Brilioth has passed on to other scholars certain conclusions about Luther's work; conservative, unclear, and by direct comparison with the canon of the mass, the concept of knife-work or violent treatment, without any constructive thought. But not only have Brilioth's conclusions on Luther been repeated in so many liturgical studies; they have been repeated without question, and usually without any reference to his criteria—the five motifs—which were his frame of reference. There is nothing sacrosanct about Brilioth's five motifs, useful as they might be. The New Testament narratives have suggested other motifs to other scholars. For example, Geoffrey Wainwright, in *Eucharist and Eschatology,* organizes his discussion on the eucharist around three basic images—the messianic feast; the advent of Christ; and the first fruits of the Kingdom.[4] I. Howard Marshall chooses a looser pattern—the Old Testament background, the death of Jesus, the risen Lord, the heavenly banquet, and the Church's meal, and uses these to offer principles for contemporary practice.[5] There is no necessity to follow Brilioth's motifs, and therefore, without those motifs, there is no need to reach his conclusions on Luther. Simply to repeat his views without reference to his criteria, and to present them as established conclusions of liturgical scholarship is highly misleading.

---

[1] *Ibid.,* p.117. [2] *Ibid.,* p.120. [3] *Ibid.,* pp.123-4.
[4] G. Wainwright *Eucharist and Eschatology* (Epworth, London, 1971).
[5] I. Howard Marshall *Last Supper and Lord's Supper* (Paternoster, Exeter, 1980).

Vilmos Vajta's Luther on Worship

A number of the more recent studies cited above have supplemented the views of Brilioth with those of Vilmos Vajta, whose *Die Theologie des Gottesdienstes bei Luther* (Stockholm 1952, Gottingen 1954), has been made more accessible to English-speaking students in the condensed version, *Luther on Worship* (Philadelphia, 1958).[1]

Vajta's study is valuable in that it attempted to escape the 'comparative liturgy' type of study which compared Luther's liturgies not only with the medieval German Catholic texts, but with the whole liturgical tradition of East and West; instead Vajta was concerned to explore the inner motives of Luther's reforms, and to set them within the framework of his theology. The English version omits vital material.

According to Vajta, Luther regarded worship as primarily a work of God, and only secondarily as work of man. As a divine institution it provides an occasion for the presentation of the word and the administration of the sacraments, and for the acceptance of these gifts by the faith of the assembled believers. Vajta examines Luther's contrast between worship and idolatry, stressing that faith is faith in a God who is God-for-us, and worship is nothing less than fellowship with God.

'Revelation and worship constitute one and the same reality: fellowship between God and man on the earthly level.'[2]

Vajta also emphasized the hitherto neglected contrast that Luther made between *'Beneficium'* and *'Sacrificium'*. God is one who gives, and not one who requires sacrifice. Luther wrote:

'For this is the true God who gives, but does not take; helps, but asks no help—in short, who does everything and gives everything, yet needs no one. And all this he does freely out of pure mercy and without merit for the unworthy and undeserving, even for the damned and lost. As such he wants to be remembered, confessed, and glorified.'[3]

Luther charged the Roman church with having made the mass a human *sacrificium* directed towards God, whereas the Gospel sacrament is a divine *beneficium* directed towards humanity, and our offering of praise and life can only be a response to God's gift. It is this contrast which explains Luther's violent criticisms of the canon of the mass, and he set about removing features of the human *sacrificium* and turning the sacrament more clearly into a divine *beneficium*. For Luther all worship is a *beneficium* of God. Vajta sees Luther's main concern in worship as restoring the word, in its written and preached form. Here the doctrine of justification is crucial:

'One could also say that righteousness is the continual subject of Luther's preaching, that is, the righteousness which Christ obtained and . . . offers to men through the preaching of the Word.'[4]

[1] E.g. G. Wainwright *Doxology*; Thompson *op. cit.* (revised edition); C. Jones et. al. *op. cit.*; Reed *op. cit.* (Revised edition); Senn, *art. cit.*

[2] References are to the English edition, *Luther on Worship* (1958) p.15.

[3] *LW* 38. 107.

[4] *op. cit.,* p.78.

15

Vajta also stresses Luther's belief in the presence of Christ in the Lord's Supper, and his view that the minister is the mouthpiece proclaiming the gift. Worship is a necessary corollary of faith; it is the means by which God through the Holy Spirit carries on his salutary work and inspires faith in men.[1] Luther's views on worship were also governed by his teaching on the priesthood of all believers, who offer to God gratitude, praise, and thanksgiving.

In a final chapter Vajta seeks to explain that Luther's reforms were also governed by the relation of Christian freedom to love of the neighbour. Faith implies liberty in all the works of man, of the law, and therewith of liturgical forms too.[2] But love of the neighbour is equally important. The weak in faith needed a form of service which would provide for their edification, yet without being bound to a single pattern. The choice of forms is not a matter of personal preference, but must depend on the need of our fellows. The liturgical choice of the 'outer man', his decision for or against certain forms, should be dictated by the need of others. Thus Vajta explains:

'Luther's "liturgical conservatism" must be seen against this background. . . . He limited himself to those liturgical forms which had come from the medieval church, and created no novel rites or appointments. This conservatism is hardly surprising. It springs from his concern for others.'[3]

Vajta's study is a useful and important work in that it serves to emphasize that Luther's liturgical work cannot be separated from the Reformer's theology, and cannot be adequately assessed without recourse to that theology. However, Vajta seems to have failed to rescue Luther from the charge of conservatism—it is excused on account of love of the neighbour—, and furthermore he gives the impression that Luther was working with many unrelated theological concepts, with no clear overall policy. Vajta did not intend to apply his appraisal of Luther's theology of worship to the actual forms; indeed, that task was to be left to others. However, those English studies which have used Vajta seem to have only partially understood his purpose. They have indicated that Luther did have a theology of worship, but have failed to apply Vajta's insights to the actual forms. The result is that Vajta has been used to supplement Brilioth rather than as a basis for a fresh appraisal of Luther's forms. And the charge of 'conservatism' is upheld.

Reservations
There are a number of reasons for hesitating over the apparent consensus opinion that in liturgical reforms, Luther was conservative, and that his work on the canon of the mass was some sort of careless knife-work. To begin with, it is difficult to know exactly what the word 'conservative' means in this context, and with what Luther's reforms are being compared. Those Reformers who anticipated Luther's reforms— Karlstadt, Kantz, Munzer—all drew out the implications of Luther's

[1] *Ibid.*, p.143.
[2] *Ibid.*, p.171.
[3] *Ibid.*, p.181.

16

sermon on the *Blessed Sacrament of the Holy and True Body of Christ* (1519), and the *Babylonian Captivity* (1520). When Luther's work is compared with the work of these Reformers, it could be argued that Kantz was the most conservative because, although his mass was in German, he felt obliged to compose an evangelical equivalent to the canon of the mass. Equally, Zwingli's *De Canone Epicheiresis* (1523), which in place of the canon had four lengthy Latin prayers, and Theobald Schwartz's Strasbourg Mass of 1524 which had a substitute canon, might be considered 'creative', but could also be described as 'conservative' in comparison to a 'radical' Farel.[1] It is true that while the medieval Western rite remains the paradigm, in comparison with Zwingli's rite of 1525 and the later work of Oecolampadius, Luther looks timid and unadventurous. But no more so than Cranmer. Cranmer's transposition of the canon into a protestant key in 1549, while reflecting a remarkable theological and literary skill, is 'conservative' in that his new canon follows the pattern of the old canon reasonably closely. It may be that comparative liturgy is not the best means of establishing whether or not a Reformation rite is conservative or radical.

It is equally questionable as to whether 'violent knife' terminology is at all justifiable in describing Luther's reform of the canon; nor are 'impatience' and 'ineptitude' appropriate. It is certainly true that when Luther is on the attack, he is violent. V. H. H. Green comments that in the dispute with Erasmus, whereas Erasmus used a rapier, Luther used a cudgel.[2] Certainly Luther could use violent language about the canon.[3] But there is another important side to Luther. Green concedes that Luther's mind 'was perhaps less incisive and his administrative genius less marked than that of John Calvin, and his general outlook more old-fashioned', but he stresses that 'profound emotion and spiritual sensitivity combined with penetrating judgment, deep biblical scholarship and intellectual power to make him the most prominent spiritual leader of his time'.[4] Gordon Rupp also observes that Luther was not the loud-mouthed beer-swilling German (that was Eck), nor an angry young man (that was Karlstadt and Munzer); how easy it is to miss the warm gentle eyes, and the small neat handwriting.[5] Indeed, Luther was a skilful and forceful theologian, and a great hymn writer, and therefore, so one would have thought, no more inept at reforming liturgy than, for instance, Martin Bucer or Oecolampadius. Rupp goes so far as to suggest that Luther 'could shape a liturgy as well as Thomas Cranmer'.[6] Perhaps, therefore, the ineptitude and impatience lie not so much with Luther as with those liturgical scholars who have been content to repeat Brilioth's views, and who have failed to investigate Luther himself.

[1] For these Reformers see, E. G. Rupp *Patterns of Reformation* (Epworth, London, 1969); H. O. Old *The Patristic Roots of Reformed Worship* (Theologischer Verlag, Zurich, 1975).
[2] V. H. H. Green *Luther and the Reformation* (Batsford, London, 1964) p.157.
[3] See below (pp.25 and 30f.).
[4] Green *op. cit.*, p.196.
[5] E. G. Rupp *Luther's Progress to the Diet of Worms 1521* (S.C.M., London, 1951), pp.64, 105; *The Righteousness of God* (Hodder and Stoughton, London, 1953[1]), p.352.
[6] Rupp, *Diet* p.105.

2. ANOTHER APPROACH: LUTHER AND JUSTIFICATION

In his work, *The Theology of Martin Luther*, H. H. Kramm made the following observation concerning a correct understanding of Luther:

'If we want to understand Luther's activities as a reformer, we have to note these two principles:

(1) The experience that man is saved by grace alone or by faith alone, is Luther's fundamental experience, the unalterable starting point of all his thinking and teaching.

(2) If this doctrine is contradicted by any other authority, Luther is quite definitely convinced that not he but his authority is wrong. Not for a single moment does he doubt the infallible truth of his doctrine and experience on justification.'[1]

While pedagogical reasons, and concern for the weak in faith did undoubtedly play a part in Luther's liturgical reforms, his objection to the canon of the mass springs directly from this 'unalterable starting point'. When it is realized that for Luther, the word or gospel is about justification and forgiveness, and the sacraments are simply the word in action, or signs which accompany the word, then it becomes possible to suggest that the rationale of the reform of the canon is to be sought in this pivotal point of all his theology, namely, justification—by grace, through faith, for Christ's sake.

Justification as the Pivotal Point of Theology and Doctrine
Luther was primarily an exegete and a preacher, and his theology was basically an attempt to interpret Scripture, for it 'alone is the true Lord and master of all writings and doctrine on earth'.[2] But for Luther the key which unlocks Scripture—therefore all theology—is the doctrine of justification. This doctrine is the summary of Christian doctrine, and the sun which illuminates God's holy church. It is the unique possession of Christianity, and to lose this doctrine is to lose Christ and the church. In the *Smalcald Articles* (1537) Luther warned:

'The first and chief article is this, that Jesus Christ, our God and Lord, "was put to death for our trespasses and raised again for our justification" (Rom. 4. 25). . . . Nothing in this article can be given up or compromised, even if heaven and earth and things temporal should be destroyed. . . . On this article rests all that we teach and practice against the pope, the devil, and the world.'[3]

The personal importance of the discovery of justification for Luther should not be underestimated. In the Preface to his Latin works of 1545, he wrote:

'Meanwhile, I had already during that year returned to interpret the Psalter anew. I had confidence in the fact that I was more skilful, after I had lectured in the university on St. Paul's Epistles to the Romans, to the Galatians, and the one to the Hebrews. I had indeed been captured with an extraordinary ardor for understanding Paul in the Epistle to the Romans. But up till then it was not the cold blood about the heart, but a single word in Chapter 1 (17), "In it the righteousness of God is revealed", that

---

[1] H. H. Kramm *The Theology of Martin Luther* (James Clarke, London, 1947) pp.24-25. Cf. E. G. Rupp *The Righteousness of God*, p.126.

[2] *LW* 32.11-12.

[3] T. G. Tappert *The Book of Concord* (Muhlenberg, Philadelphia, 1959) p.292.

had stood in the way. For I hated that word "righteousness of God", which according to the use of custom of all the teachers, I had been taught to understand philosophically regarding the formal or active righteousness, as they called it, with which God is righteous and punishes the unrighteous sinner.

Though I lived as a monk without reproach, I felt that I was a sinner before God with an extremely disturbed conscience. I could not believe that he was placated by my satisfaction. I did not love, yes, I hated that righteous God who punishes sinners, and secretly, if not blasphemously, certainly murmuring greatly, I was angry with God, and said, "As if, indeed, it is not enough, that miserable sinners, eternally lost through original sin, are crushed by every kind of calamity by the law of the decalogue, without having God add pain to pain by the gospel and also by the gospel threatening us with his righteousness and wrath!" Thus I raged with a fierce and troubled conscience. Nevertheless, I beat importunately upon Paul at that place, most ardently desiring to know what St. Paul wanted.

At last, by the mercy of God, meditating day and night, I gave heed to the context of the words, namely, "In it the righteousness of God is revealed, as it is written, 'He who through faith is righteous shall live'". There I began to understand that the righteousness of God is that by which the righteous lives by a gift of God, namely by faith. And this is the meaning: the righteousness of God is revealed by the gospel, namely, the passive righteousness which the merciful God justifies us by faith, as it is written, "He who through faith is righteous shall live". Here I felt that I was altogether born again and had entered paradise itself through open gates. There a totally other face of the entire Scripture showed itself to me. Thereupon I ran through the Scriptures from memory. I also found in other terms an analogy, as, the work of God, that is, what God does in us, the power of God, with which he makes us strong, the wisdom of God, with which he makes us wise, the strength of God, the salvation of God, the glory of God.'[1]

Elsewhere he wrote:
'Justice, i.e. grace. This word I learned with much sweat. They used to expound justice as the truth of God which punishes the damned, mercy as that which saves believers. A dangerous opinion which arouses a secret hatred of the heart against God, so that it is terrified when he is so much as named. Justice is that which the Father does when he favours us, with which he justifies, or the gift with which he takes away our sins.'[2]

Although Heinrich Denifle tried to show that Luther had either misunderstood or deliberately misrepresented the doctors of the

[1] LW 34.336-337.
[2] Otto Scheel, Dokumente zu Luthers Entwicklung, Tübingen 1929, quoted in Rupp, The Righteousness of God, p.126.

Western Church, Luther's integrity has been vindicated.[1] He seems to have come to a new understanding of the 'Justice of God' during his lectures on the Psalms in 1514.[2]

While at first sight the importance Luther attached to justification may seem out of all proportion, it is more understandable when it is realized that for Luther 'justification', 'the word', 'Jesus Christ', and 'the gospel', are bound together inseparably, and are almost interchangeable terms. The doctrine of Christ is also described as the essence of all Christian knowledge; it is the decisive element of Christianity which distinguishes it from all other religions; it is the criterion by which all matters of doctrine and life are to be judged.[3] Christ is the Lord and Author of Scripture.[4] In his reply to Erasmus', *On Bondage of the Will* (1525), Luther asserted:

> 'For what still sublimer thing can remain hidden in the Scriptures, now that the seals have been broken, the stone rolled from the door of the sepulchre (Matt. 27.11; 28.2), and the supreme mystery brought to light namely, that Christ the Son of God has been made man, that God is three and one, that Christ has suffered for us and is to reign eternally? Are not these things known and sung even in the highways and byways? Take Christ out of the Scriptures, and what will you find left in them?'[5]

For Luther, Scripture must be interpreted Christocentrically, which means gospel-centred interpretation, understood in terms of the gospel of justification by faith alone. Paul Althaus rightly stresses that for the Wittenberg reformer, 'Christ' means the gospel of that free mercy of God in Christ on which alone man's salvation depends.[6]

The close link between gospel, Christ, and justification, is evident in Luther's comments on Romans. In the *Scholia* (1.3-4) he explains:

> *The Gospel* is not only what Matthew, Mark, Luke and John have written. This is clear enough from this passage. For it states expressly that the Gospel is the Word concerning the Son of God, who became flesh, suffered, and was glorified. Therefore, no matter who writes and teaches it, whether Matthew or Thomas, and no matter in what words or tongues, it is the same Gospel of God.'[7]

And on verse 17,

> 'The Righteousness of God is revealed. In human teachings the righteousness of man is revealed and taught, that is, who is and becomes righteous before himself and before other people and how this takes place. Only in the Gospel is the righteousness of God revealed (that is, who is and becomes righteous before God and how this takes place) by faith alone, by which the Word of

---

[1] Rup, *ibid.,* pp.123ff.

[2] *Ibid., pp.136-7.*

[3] *LW* 21.59.

[4] *LW* 26.295.

[5] *LW* 33.25-26.

[6] P. Althaus, *The Theology of Martin Luther* (ET, Fortress Press, Philadelphia, 1966) p.79.

[7] *LW* 21.148-149.

God is believed, as it is written in the last chapter of Mark (16.16):
"He who believes and is baptized will be saved; but he who does
not believe will be condemned". For the righteousness of God is
the cause of salvation.'[1]

Luther found St. Paul to have most clearly understood and expressed
the gospel, and he could describe the Epistle to the Romans as a
'bright light, almost sufficient to illuminate the entire holy Scriptures',
that is, to shed light on the Old and New Testaments.[2] It is precisely on
these grounds that Luther was daring enough in 1522 to reorganize the
canon of Scripture. Following comments by the Fathers, Luther applied
the criterion of justification to place James, Jude, Hebrews, and
Revelation, in a sub-category. All genuine books agree in preaching
Christ, and these four books, although they frequently mentioned the
word Christ—and in the case of Hebrews, witnessed to the priestly
office of Christ—did not proclaim the gospel of justification. It is
reasonable to infer that if it was a guiding principle important enough
to suggest the rearrangement of the canon of Scripture, it was equally
crucial in the reform of liturgy, including the canon of the mass.

Justification and Liturgy
It is true, as Vajta has explained, that freedom was an important
element in Luther's liturgical reforms. However, for Luther Christian
freedom is itself an important corollary of justification. Since Christ is
the end of the law, the law is abrogated for the justified man, and he is
free from the demands, from the compulsion, from the accusation and
the condemnation of the law. He has been transferred from the
kingdom of the law into Christ's kingdom.[3] But this freedom of the law
applies equally to ecclesiastical laws and impositions. Luther's
criticism of the ceremonies and ceremonial law should be seen in this
context. The Reformer's advice on liturgy is therefore cautious, with the
'shall' rubric replaced by 'may'. For example, in his advice to the
congregation at Leisnig we find repeated exhortations to freedom:
'. . . as may seem most suitable . . . that is a matter of choice . . . or
the preacher may use his own judgment.'[4]

Thus, in *FM*,
'Nonetheless, I have no intention of cramping anyone's freedom
or of introducing a law that might lead to superstition . . .'[5]

Equally true is Luther's concern for love of the neighbour and the weak.
His hesitancy in reform was for this reason: 'For I have been hesitant
and fearful, partly because of the weak in faith'.[6] Furthermore, love for
the neighbour is important: I should become a Christ to my neighbour
and be for him what Christ is for me. This principle is to be followed in
all of life and includes everything that is 'necessary, useful and a
blessing' to my neighbour.[7] Again;
'God is satisfied with my faith . . . Therefore he wants me to do my
works to benefit my neighbor . . . he doesn't need my works at all

---

[1] *LW* 25.151. [2] *LW* 35.366. [3] Althaus, *op. cit.*, p.266.
[4] *LW* 53.11, *passim*. [5] *LW* 53.25. cf. *LW* 53.61.
[6] *LW* 53.19. [7] *LW* 31.367ff.

. . . God is rich enough himself without me and without my works. He lets me live on earth, however, so that I may show the same kind of friendship to my neighbor that God has graciously shown to me . . . Thus God fuses the two commandments into each other so that there is only one work and only one love. Whatever we do for our neighbor by preaching, teaching, clothing him, and feeding him is all done to Christ himself.'[1]

Faith becomes incarnate in the works of love, and liturgical changes need to take this into account. But as Martin E. Marty stresses:

'For Luther justification was prior to love, which he described as the effect and fruit of faith, the spirit, and justification; it was not an arbitrary ornament.'[2]

Indeed, Christian freedom and love of the neighbour spring from justification, and while Luther takes these latter things into account, worship and liturgical forms are governed not primarily by these, but by the gospel, and therefore by the doctrine of justification. While it is true that Luther classed liturgical ceremonies as things indifferent (*adiaphora*), Pelikan points out that this did not mean, as Brilioth took it to mean, that Luther himself was indifferent to liturgy and liturgical forms.[3] Luther simply meant that precise liturgical forms and ceremonies had not been prescribed in detail in the gospel. Christ's example is not binding on us, except by express command. Nevertheless, in his discourse on ceremonies (1520) with reference to Psalm 14, Luther pointed out that there is no public worship without forms. Liturgical forms should be used as a framework for the proclamation of the gospel. But what *is* binding is the word of God. The ultimate pivotal point of liturgy, as with all Luther's theology, was not freedom or the needs of our neighbour, but God's word. Ronald Feuerhahn admirably makes this point with reference to a letter to Nicholas Hausmann. He writes:

'These essentials, furthermore, were firmly grounded in the Word. We need only recall that litany-like repetition from the letter to Hausmann: "only with the Word . . . with the Word . . .with the Word . . . only with the Word . . . by the Word." These are the words of the subject who stood before his emperor and declared that his conscience was "captive to the Word". This reference to the Word of God, the Word dynamic in preaching as well as the Scriptures, always active and powerful, that Word is basic to our understanding of Luther.'[3]

According to Luther, it is in worship that the Christian receives primarily the Word of God's promise, and chiefly the promise of forgiveness; worship is an occasion when a man hears about justification. Reading Scripture was important, for it proclaimed the

---

[1] *WA* 20.513.

[2] Martin E. Marty 'Luther on Ethics: Man Free and Slave' in Heino O. Kadai (ed.) *Accents in Luther's Theology* Concordia, St. Louis and London, 1967) p.224.

[3] Jaroslav J. Pelikan 'Luther and the Liturgy' in *More About Luther* (Martin Luther Lectures Vol. 2, Luther College Press, Decorah, Iowa, 1958) pp.3-62, p.5 and *passim*.

[4] Ronald R. Feuerhahn, *Luther's Mass. Origin, Content and Impact 1521-1529*, (M.Phil. Thesis, Cambridge University, 1980) pp.24-25.

gospel; but the oral proclamation of preaching is the proper form of the word. Originally, the gospel was not a book, but a sermon, and the church not a *Federhaus* (pen (quill)-house), but a *Mundhaus* (mouth-house).[1] For Luther, 'preaching' means preaching Christ, which in turn means proclaiming that the crucified and risen Christ is the Saviour and that the salvation he brings is received through faith alone.

The sacraments were, according to Luther, signs which accompanied the word:

> 'We may learn from this that in every promise of God two things are presented to us, the word and the sign, so that we are to understand the word to be the testament, but the sign to be the sacrament. Thus, in the mass, the word of Christ is the testament, and the bread and wine are the sacrament.'[2]

For this, regarding baptism and the eucharist, Luther could appeal to St. Augustine, *'Accedat verbum ad elementum et fit sacramentum'.*[3] However, the word is greater than the sign,[4] and it is the word which makes the sign a sacrament. However, whereas the preaching of the word was directed to all, the sacraments convey the content of the word to a particular individual:

> 'When I preach his death, it is in a public sermon in the congregation, in which I am addressing myself to no one individually; whoever grasps it, grasps it. But when I distribute the sacrament, I designate it for the individual who is receiving it; I give him Christ's body and blood that he may have forgiveness of sins, obtained through his death, and preached in the congregation. This is something more than the congregational sermon; for although the same thing is present in the sermon as in the sacrament, here there is the advantage that it is directed at definite individuals. In the sermon one does not point out or portray any particular person, but in the sacrament it is given to you and to me in particular, so that the sermon comes to be our own.'[1]

In the word and sacrament, therefore, the worshipper is confronted with the good news of justification. It is to be expected, therefore, that liturgical forms will be concerned to convey this; if they contradict it, then they must be reformed accordingly.

This theological approach to liturgical reforms can be illustrated from Luther's *Taufbüchlein.*[2] In his consideration of baptism, Luther was at pains to emphasize two aspects: the objectivity of God's declaration of forgiveness and remission of sins, and the apprehension of this which comes by faith and is symbolized in baptism. Baptism was the outward sign of justification. Thus in *The Holy and Blessed Sacrament of Baptism* (1519) Luther wrote:

> 'the significance of baptism is a blessed dying unto sin and a resurrection in the grace of God, so that the old man, conceived

---

[1] *WA* 10.2. [2] *LW* 36.44. [3] Large Catechism, *Book of Concord*, pp.438, 448.
[4] *LW* 35.91. [5] *LW* 36.348. [6] Bryan D. Spinks, 'Luther's Taufbüchlein'.

and born in sin, is there drowned, and a new man, born in grace, comes forth and rises. .... Through this spiritual birth he is a child of grace and a justified person.'[1]

Indeed, baptism is the sacrament of justification, bringing forth salvation, redemption from sin, liberation from the devil, and leading to Christ. Nevertheless, it is not the external ceremony itself which justifies men, for unless faith is present, baptism profits nothing.[2] However, Luther was careful to avoid any charge of subjectivity, for he emphasized that this faith was faith in the promise of God to forgive sins. Thus he could write:

'My faith does not make the baptism but rather receives baptism, no matter whether the person baptized believes or not; for baptism is not dependent upon my faith but upon God's word.'[3]

Regarding the administration of this sacrament, Luther emphasized both the divine and human aspects. First the divine word which was added to the water. By this Luther did not have in mind a blessing of the water, but the divine promise (Mark 16,16) and the authority to baptize in the three-fold name. The divine promise guaranteed the reality of forgiveness, and the authority of Matthew 28.19 indicated that it was not the minister who baptized, but God himself. For Luther, in the baptismal formula, it was God himself proclaiming forgiveness. With this went the sign, by which the promise was pledged, and by which man accepted the divine forgiveness and justification. When the minister immersed the candidate in the water, this signified death, and when he drew him out, it signified life. 'Baptism then, signified two things—death and resurrection, that is, full and complete justification'.[4]

In an Epilogue to his first *Taufbüchlein,* Luther readily admitted that he did not wish to make great alterations, both for the sake of tender consciences (love of the neighbour), and also to escape the charge of inventing a new baptism. Nevertheless, Luther stated that the liturgy was in need of improvement, because careless authors had obscured 'the glory of baptism'. Thus he retained such things as putting salt in the infant's mouth, spittle and clay on the ears and nose, and anointing with oil, because they were human ceremonies which added nothing to baptism, and since they were not forbidden in Scripture, were things indifferent. On the other hand, the blessing of the water was one of the elements that were removed, because all that was needed was the Divine Word, and a petition for consecration suggested lack of faith in the power of God's Word; ultimately, it was to distrust God. In the 1526 *Taufbüchlein* the human ceremonies were removed which 'men have added to embellish baptism'. [5] In this order, the officiant demands the unclean spirit to give way to the Holy Spirit. The child receives the cross on its forehead and breast, a sign of the cost of the redemption now being offered. A prayer asked for regeneration, followed by the

---

[1] *LW* 25.30.
[2] *LW* 36.59.
[3] *LW* 5[1].186 (Sermons on Catechism 1528).
[4] *LW* 36.67.
[5] *LW* 53.102.

'flood prayer', with the Old Testament 'types' of justification. Again the unclean spirit is called out. Then followed the Gospel, the Lord's Prayer, the renunciations, confession of faith, and baptism in the name of the Trinity. A white robe was still put on the infant, not simply because it was a custom, but because it symbolized the new life of the justified person.

That the same theological concern—justification—underlies Luther's reform of the canon of the mass is clearly stated by Luther himself. In the Smalcald Articles (1537). Referring back to the article on justification, Luther wrote:

'The Mass in the papacy must be regarded as the greatest and most horrible abomination because it runs into direct and violent conflict with this [i.e. the article on justification] fundamental article.'[1]

And again,
'The Mass is and can be nothing else than a human work, even a work of evil scoundrels (as the canon and all books on the subject declare), for by means of the Mass men try to reconcile themselves and others to God and obtain and merit grace and the forgiveness of sins. It is observed for this purpose when it best observed. What other purpose could it have? Therefore, it should be condemned and must be abolished because it is a direct contradiction to the fundamental article . . .'[2]

It is with the conviction that justification is the key to Luther's reform of the canon that we shall proceed to examine his proposals in more detail.

[1] Book of Concord, p.293.
[2] Ibid., pp.293-4 (my italics).

ADDITIONAL BIBLIOGRAPHY

In addition to the works cited in the study, the following are also useful:

Walter E. Buszin, 'Luther on Music' in Musical Quarterly,32:1 (1946), pp.80-97.
Edward Trail Horn, 'Luther on the Principles and Order of Christian Worship' in Lutheran Church Review 11 (1892), pp.301-344.
C. J. Kiefer 'Luther and Hymnology' in Lutheran Church Review 32 (1913) pp.237-248.
J. F. Kruegar, 'Liturgical Worship in Wittenberg From 1520-1530', in Lutheran Church Quarterly 4(1931), pp,292-303.
E. Reim 'The Liturgical Crisis in Wittenberg, 1524' in Concordia Theological Monthly 20(1949), pp.284-292.
G. Rupp, 'Andrew Karlstadt and Reformation Puritanism' in Journal of Theological Studies NS 10(1959), pp.308-326.
Frank C. Senn 'Luther's German Mass—A Sixteenth Century Folk Service', in Journal of Church Music 18.8. (1976), pp.2-6.

3. LUTHER'S REFORM OF THE CANON OF THE MASS

The Canon of the Mass

The traditional text of the canon with which the Reformers were aquainted had been fairly uniform since about A.D. 700, though the details of development to that date remain obscure. The earliest evidence for the structure of the eucharistic prayer at Rome is found in Justin Martyr's *First Apology* and the *Apostolic Tradition* attributed to Hippolytus.[1] It seems to have remained fluid up to the time of Gregory the Great, and it may be presumed that it originally possessed a long beginning, with creation and Christological passages, which has since disappeared; perhaps the oldest proper prefaces preserve some phrases of what was said on the oldest feast, as an inset in the wider Christological passage.[2] The text given by St. Ambrose in *De Sacramentis IV* appears to be parallel to the contemporary Roman usage. The text of the canon as it is preserved in the old Gelasian, *codex Vat.Reginensis lat.316*[3], is prefaced by the rubric *'Incipit canon actionis',* and there follows at once the introductory dialogue, 'Sursum corda', the Sanctus, Te igitur, and so on. It is possible that in the Roman tradition the Sanctus with its introduction is an interpolation dating from the fifth century.[4] If the Sanctus is regarded as an interpolation, then according to E. C. Ratcliff and G. G. Willis, Te igitur will be seen to carry on the thought of the preface. The sequence is 'Vere dignum et justum est . . . tibi gratias agere . . . te igitur . . . supplices rogamus . . . uti accepta hebeas . . . haec dona'; sacrifice is here conceived in accordance with the Irenaean tradition.[5] The lists of apostles, saints and martyrs, together with the Memento Domine and Memento etiam, perhaps once recited by the deacon, and only in his absence by the celebrant, and so becoming part of the canon[6], seem to have entered during this period, though according to the study of Keifer, they represent a quite logical development of the oblation-supplication thought of the canon.[7] The Hanc igitur commended the offerers to God, and the Quam oblationem asked God to bless, ratify and accept the oblation of bread and wine, that it might be the body and blood of Christ. This led into the words of institution, Qui pridie and Simili modo, much of which seems to have been derived from the

[1] But for the view that the *Apostolic Ttradition* represents Alexandrine usage, see J. M. Hanssens *La Liturgie d'Hippolyte,* OCA 155, (Pont. Institutum Orientalium Studiorum, Rome, 1959 and 1965).

[2] A. H. Couratin and the late E. C. Ratcliff, 'The Early Roman Canon Missae' in *Journal of Ecclesiastical History* 20 (1969), pp.211-224, p.217.

[3] L. C. Mohlberg, *Liber Sacramentorum Romanae Ecclesiae Ordinis anni circuli* (Herder, Rome, 1960) pp.183-186.

[4] L. Chavoutier, 'Un *Libellus* Pseudo-Ambrosien sur le Saint-Esprit', in *Sacris Erudiri* 11(1960), pp.180-191.

[5] E. C. Ratcliff, 'Christian Worship and Liturgy', in ed. K. E. Kirk, *The Study of Theology,* (Hodder and Stoughton, London, 1939) p.443; G. G. Willis, *Essays in Early Roman Liturgy* (Alcuin/SPCK, London, 1964) p.124.

[6] A. H. Couratin and the late E. C. Ratcliff, *art. cit*; E. C. Ratcliff in Kirk, *op. cit.,* p.441; G. G. Willis, *op. cit.,* p.38.

[7] Ralph A. Keifer, 'The Unity of the Roman Canon: An Examination of its unique Structure', in *SL* 11(1976), pp.39-58.

old Latin version of Matthew 26.26-28.[1] Then followed the anamnesis, Unde et memores, offering the consecrated elements to God. The prayer Supra quae asked God to accept the new covenant, and the Supplices te asked that the oblation might be carried to the heavenly altar, and also for benefits for the communicants. After the Memento etiam and Nobis quoque came the doxology and the final Amen. By A.D. 700 the canon seems to have reached its traditional form, only receiving minor alterations at the hands of Alcuin of York[2], or at least, during the Carolingian reform. From the eighth century manuscripts it is clear that it was thought to begin *after* the Preface and Sanctus with Te igitur, the 'T' of which was given great prominence.[3] The Sursum corda-Sanctus thus came to be regarded as a preliminary to the canon, and not part of it. Since 1474 the canon was printed in paragraphs, marked with initial letters, and divided by rubrics. The paragraphs Communicantes, Hanc igitur, Supplices te, Memento etiam, and Nobis quoque had a conclusion 'Per (eundum) Christum Dominum nostrum', and to this was added Amen in every case except the last.[4] It was in this latter form that it was known to the Reformers.

Although modern liturgical scholarship has helped to clarify some points of history of the canon of the mass, this eucharistic prayer still remains an enigma. The note of sacrifice, and intercession for others, may well be an earlier feature of eucharistic prayers than has hitherto been admitted.[5] Nevertheless, the sacrificial note in this Roman eucharistic prayer is rather pronounced, and most, if not all, of the Reformation Fathers could assent to Thomas Becon's description:

'It is a hotch-potch; . . . It is a very beggar's cloak, cobbled, clouted and patched with a multitude of popish rags.'[6]

Luther, too, was not more polite about this ancient eucharistic prayer; it was an 'abominable concoction drawn from everyone's sewer and cesspool'.[7]

Luther on the Eucharist: Testament, not Sacrifice
For Luther, God's justice is that he has forgiven us, though we have done nothing to deserve it; this forgiveness is sealed in the one complete sacrifice of Christ on the cross. What is required of men is

[1] E. C. Ratcliff, 'The Institution Narrative of the Roman Canon Missae: Its beginnings and early background', in *Studia Patristica* II,pp.64-82, *Texte und Untersuchungen* 64, Berlin 1957.

[2] Bernard Botte *Le Canon De La Messe Romaine* (Abbaye du Mont César, Louvain, 1935) pp.15-17.

[3] Rosamund McKitterick, *The Frankish Church and the Carolingian Reforms, 789-895* (Royal Historical Society, London, 1977) p.142.

[4] G. G. Willis, *op. cit.*, pp.121ff.

[5] E.g. Strasbourg Papyrus. See G. J. Cuming, 'The Anaphora of St. Mark, A Study in Development', forthcoming in *Le Muséon*; W. H. Bates, 'Thanksgiving and Intercession in the Liturgy of St. Mark', in Bryan D. Spinks, (ed.), *The Sacrifice of Praise* (C.L.V., Rome, 1981); H. A. J. Wegman, 'Une Anaphore Incomplète?', in R. Van Den Broek and M. Vermaseren, in *Studies in Gnosticism and Hellenistic Religions* (E. J. Brill, Leiden, 1981).

[6] *Prayers and other pieces of Thomas Becon* (Chaplain to Archbishop Cranmer), (Parker Society, Cambridge, 1844) p.266.

[7] *LW* 53.21.

that they believe this. Since Luther saw the sacraments as signs accompanying the word; the eucharist, like baptism, was a sign of the word which proclaims justification. In fact, the eucharist could be described as a testament of forgiveness.

Luther first expounded this idea of the eucharist as testament in his lectures on Hebrews in 1514. In his study of the meaning of testament in the young Luther, Kenneth Hagen writes:

'Throughout his *Lectures on Hebrews* Luther uses the concept of the Eucharist as a testament rather than a sacrifice. This is not to say that testament and sacrifice are mutually exclusive categories. it is rather that Luther's discussion of the Eucharist in terms of a testament leads him to different conclusions from those of medieval exegetes who discuss it in terms of a sacrifice.'[1]

Hagen shows that whereas the medieval exegetes, commenting on Hebrews 8.6, regarded the content of the New Testament as the promise of eternal life, Luther broke new ground in explaining the promise as being *the forgiveness of sins* as well as eternal life.[2] Again, whereas the medieval exegetes discussed the eucharist in terms of sacrifice when commenting on Hebrews 10.1-3, Luther broke new ground when he discussed the eucharist in relation to Hebrews 9.17, explaining it not as a sacrifice, but as a testament.[3] Luther admits that he took over the idea of testament from St. John Chrysostom, but he criticizes Chrysostom for failing to discuss the question of what Christ bequeathed in his testament.[4] For Luther, it is forgiveness, of which the bread and wine at the eucharist are the seal. So commenting on Hebrews 9.14, Luther wrote:

'No law, no work, in fact nothing at all can effect this purity, except the blood of Christ alone, and not even Christ's blood unless a man in his heart believes that it was poured out for the forgiveness of sins. Thus one must believe him who made the testament. "This is my blood which is poured out for the forgiveness of sins" (Matt. 26.28).'[5]

This teaching is clarified in *A Treatise on the New Testament* (1520). Luther explained that there are many parts to a testament; the testator—Christ; the heirs—Christians; the testament—the words of Christ in the institution; the seal, or token—the bread and wine; and the bequeathed blessings—forgiveness of sins and eternal life.[6] in his early work Luther admitted that the words 'offertory' and 'sacrifice' might legitimately be used of the mass, but only because of the food which was gathered, and the prayer in which God was thanked and the food blessed, and not because of the sacrament which was a testament.[7] Any good work or offering to God which was connected with petition for forgiveness was untenable, because this would imply

---

[1] Kenneth Hagen *A Theology of Testament in the Young Luther. The Lectures on Hebrews* (E. J. Brill, Leiden, 1974) pp.112-3.
[2] *Ibid.*, p.109. [3] *Ibid.*, p.111. [4] *Ibid.*, p. 109.
[5] *WA* 57 III 207-208. [6] *LW* 35.86-87. [7] *LW* 35.94ff.

that Christ's single sacrifice was not altogether complete for the redemption of men. In fact, any such offering would be tantamount to re-sacrificing Christ, by trying to gain that which had already been gained by Christ. There was a sacrifice at the eucharist—of prayer, praise, and thanksgiving; but we do not offer Christ as a sacrifice, because he offers us.[1] Since the eucharist is a testament, it is a gift of God to us, and is something which we receive; it is not a sacrifice which we offer to God.[2]

Luther and the Canon

It was from the standpoint that the eucharist is a testament that Luther approached the canon. His attack on the mass as a sacrifice was answered by his opponents with reference to the wording of the canon. This explains Luther's suspicions which were already apparent in the *Babylonian Captivity of the Church* (1520).

'Now there is yet a second stumbling block that must be removed, and this is much greater and the most dangerous of all. It is the common belief that the mass is a sacrifice, which is offered to God. Even the words of the canon seem to imply this, when they speak of "these gifts, these presents, these holy sacrifices", and further on "this offering". Prayer is also made, in so many words, "that the sacrifice may be accepted even as the sacrifice of Abel", etc. Hence Christ is termed "the sacrifice of the altar".'[3]

Over against this, Luther insisted, must be set the words and example of Christ, which showed that the mass was a promise or testament. However, his suspicions grew. In his work of the following year, *The Misuse of the Mass,* he emphasized that according to Scripture, there are only two sacrifices, the sacrifice of the cross (Heb. 10.10), and the sacrifice of praise (Heb. 13.15). But his opponents 'throw up' the secret mass, which they call the canon:

'In it there are the words: "these gifts, holy and unspotted sacrifices", and further on: "a holy offering, a pure offering and an unspotted offering, etc".'[4]

But clearly, Luther now saw this to be an affront to the gospel of Christ:

'If they say: The words in the canon are clear and manifest and need no glosses, then we in return also say: The words of the gospel are clear and plain and need no glosses. . . . We say that the canon, because it is a human word and work, shall yield to the gospel and give place to the Holy Spirit. . . . Because the canon was invited to the marriage feast and sat down in a place of honor, it shall now get up with shame and give place to Christ, its master, and sit in the lowest place, as it should properly have done in the beginning.'[5]

Stronger language was contained in *Receiving both Kinds* (1522):

'The second step is for the priests who celebrate mass to avoid every word in the canon and the collects which refer to sacrifice. . . .It simply must and shall be done away with, no matter who takes offence.'[6]

[1] *LW* 35.99. [2] *LW* 35.94. [3] *LW* 36.51.
[4] *LW* 36.184. [5] *LW* 36.185. [6] *LW* 36.254.

29

It emerges that, for Luther, the canon is a serious problem. It is in fact something that is incompatible with the gospel, and has in fact taken the place of the gospel. For Luther it was a question of Yahweh or Baal, the gospel or the canon. But another point also emerges; Luther began to express the view that *the entire canon must be removed.* It contains a nonsense, and is an enemy of the gospel;[1] it is an 'abominable concoction drawn from everyone's sewer and cesspool.'[2] It is the root of sacerdotalism, ecclesiastical avarice, votive masses, and money-making. Its one saving grace is that it contains the Words of Institution.[3] Nevertheless, Luther's advice is quite clear:

> 'Let us, therefore, repudiate everything that smacks of sacrifice, together with the entire canon and retain only that which is pure and holy, and so order our mass.'[4]

Any further doubts about the canon were removed by his analysis, *The Abomination of the Secret Mass* (1525), which may be summarized as follows:[5]

(1) *Te igitur.* The priest asks God to regard the wafer as so precious. Shall a little bread and wine be offered to God for him to accept on behalf of all Christendom? When these words are said, 'we offer thee this on behalf of the whole world and beseech thee that thou wilt deign to be pleased with it', it is equivalent to blaspheming and saying to God publicly before the whole world 'we have to help Christendom with bread and wine; it is a barefaced lie when you say that the blood of your Son alone is sufficient'.

(2) *Memento Domine.* Here the priest includes 'those who are here present', that they are supposed to offer with him the plain bread and wine, and he says the same thing also about those who have faith. For what purpose are these offerings made? 'For the redemption of their souls, etc.' It is the same as saying 'Those whom Christ has redeemed with his blood, that is Christians, are not redeemed and are not Christians but we will make ourselves Christians and redeem ourselves with a piece of bread and a drink of wine'.

(3) *Communicantes.* Christ instituted his body and blood as a remembrance of him and as a means of fellowship. This fool of a canon makes of it a remembrance and fellowship of the departed saints, and makes them mediators. Christ alone is the mediator.

(4) *Hanc igitur.* Again the priest offers bread and wine for Christendom.

(5) *Quam oblationem.* The foolish canon does not know itself what it is saying. It quotes from Paul's letter that the sacrifice is to become reasonable but not until it has become the body and blood of Christ. Then too it is to become accredited and blessed. It will surely please God that we should pray to him to give heed to this petition and thereby for the first time be gracious to his Son and bless him and make him acceptable—when it is really through him that we are blessed and sanctified.

[1] *LW* 36.185, 186.   [2] *LW* 53.21.   [3] *LW* 53.26.   [4] *Ibid.*   [5] *LW* 36.314-323.

(6) *Qui pridie* and *Simili modo.* The words have departed from the scriptural versions, in particular by the addition of the word *'enim',* and the laity are refused the chalice.

(7) *Unde et memores.* The priest offers up once again the Lord Christ, who offered himself only once.

(8) *Supra quae.* A blasphemy—God is asked to be pleased with the sacrifice of his Son! Christ's blood is supposed to sanctify and reconcile, but the canon tries to do this itself instead. It is an insult to parallel Christ's offering with Abel and Abraham because he fulfils theirs. And it is not true that Melchizedek sacrificed bread and wine.

(9) *Supplices te.* Now redemption is gained simply through prayer.

(10) *Memento etiam.* This part is worth money. If the dead repose in the sleep of peace, why does the canon pray that they might rest in peace?

(11) *Nobis quoque.* Here the canon wants the faithful to receive a portion with Christ.

(12) *Per ipsum.* It speaks of 'many' but only the priest in fact communicates.

In this analysis, it is clear that Luther is attacking and mocking the logic of the phraseology of the canon. But underneath this, there is a deeper issue; Luther believed the gospel to be a declaration of the love and forgiveness of God—of what God had done for us. The canon, however, is preoccupied with what we are doing for God. It was precisely this which meant that the canon was incompatible with the doctrine of justification. However much it was the intention of the canon to enter into what Christ had done, it seemed to attempt redemption in its own right.[1] This it was deleted from *FM,* and there was no chance of it reappearing in *DM.* In the letter there is no mention of it, for it had indeed been 'simply . . . done away with, no matter who takes offence'.

Luther's Reformed Canon

When compared with the canon, Luther's new 'office' (a title he uses elsewhere seemingly for the canon[2]) and consecration appear to be merely a remnant of the former: the Sursum corda and Preface (*FM* only), a new Qui pridie and Simili modo tagged on to the Preface, and the elevation during the Sanctus. However, the origin of this reform is *not* to be sought in the canon but in Luther's understanding of the eucharist. His reformed canon represents none other than a quintessence of the doctrine of justification by faith.

. . . A. The Sursum corda and Preface

In *FM* Luther retained the Sursum corda and Preface, which for modern liturgists is the classical introduction to the eucharistic prayer. However, it has already been noted above from the printed texts of the period, (and it is in Langeford's meditations), that the canon was regarded as beginning with Te igitur, and thus in Luther's day, these

---

[1] Cyprian seems to imply that the priest must imitate what Christ said and did, re-enacting the passion. See E. C. Ratcliff, 'The Institution Narrative of the Roman Canon Missae'.

[2] *LW* 35.97.

elements were not considered to be part of the canon. This partly accounts for its retention in 1523. The mention of angels and archangels was deleted since its natural connection with the Sanctus was broken.

Likewise the Sanctus, which at high mass was sung by the choir, was not regarded as part of the canon, but merely an anthem leading into it, accompanied by the sacring bell, or even with Benedictus qui venit, sung while the priest hurried silently through the canon and read the words of institution. Luther thus found a new, and arguably more fitting place for this anthem, after the words of institution (see below).

In *DM* the Sursum corda and Preface disappeared, being replaced by a paraphrase of the Lord's Prayer and a brief exhortation. There is no need to regard this as liturgical barbarism; there is evidence which suggests that Luther regarded these latter as a German equivalent, or interpretation, of the Sursum corda and Preface. To begin with, Luther wanted a German liturgy which was a proper German composition, and not simply the Latin idiom rendered awkwardly into German:

> 'I would gladly have a German mass today. I am also occupied with it. But I would very much like it to have a true German character. For to translate the Latin text and retain the Latin tone or notes has my sanction, though it doesn't sound polished or well done. Both the text and notes, accent, melody, and manner of rendering ought to grow out of the true mother tongue and its inflection, otherwise . . . it becomes an imitation, in the manner of the apes.[1]

Elsewhere he stated that a German mass would have to have a genuine style.[2] It would seem therefore, that like other Reformers[3], Luther saw Sursum corda as a kind of exhortation to the worshippers to lift their hearts and minds to heavenly things, and to give thanks to God. This could be directly achieved by a paraphrase of the Lord's Prayer, which for Luther said everything to God that needed to be said by men[4], and by direct exhortation in German to 'discern the Testament of Christ in true faith and, above all, take to heart the words wherein Christ imparts to us his body and his blood for the remission of our sins'.

. . . B. The Words of Institution

Common to both *FM* and *DM*, and central to both, were the words of institution which were preferably to be intoned. However, the centrality and prominence given to the words should not be interpreted, as Bouyer suggests, as being a pronounced medieval idea of consecration by recitation of the words, nor primarily as an expression of Luther's doctrine of the presence, commonly termed 'consubstantiation'.

Firstly, the words which Luther provided were not simply the Qui pridie and Simili modo. Luther was very critical of the words in the canon: Qui

---

[1] *LW* 40.141.   [2] *LW* 53.54.

[3] Calvin and Farel interpreted the Sursum corda in this way. See Bryan D. Spinks, *The Eucharistic Liturgy in the English Independent, or Congregational, Tradition: A Study of its changing structure and content, 1550-1974* (B.D. Thesis, Durham University, 1979).

[4] Commenting on the meaning of the conclusion of the Lord's Prayer, Luther says: It means that I should be assured that such petitions are acceptable to our heavenly Father and are heard by him, for he himself commanded us to pray like this and promised to hear us. (*Book of Concord,* p.348.)

pridie had left out 'which is for you', and had added, among others, the little word 'enim'.[1] The Simili modo spoke of all drinking, whereas in fact the cup was denied to the laity. Luther felt free to emend the text accordingly.

The importance of the words of institution for Luther is not to be questioned. In *The Adoration of the Sacrament* (1523), addressed to the Waldensians, he stated plainly that the chief and foremost thing in the sacrament was the words of Christ, 'Take and eat,' etc, for everything depended on these words.[3] Against the fanatics he emphasized that the word 'is' did not mean 'signifies', but meant that Christ was really present in his word, and in the *Babylonian Captivity* he likened the presence to that of fire in red-hot iron.[3] Luther used the doctrine of ubiquity and Ockham's definition of Being, to maintain that in the eucharistic elements the presence of God is to be apprehended.[4] His stand against Zwingli at Marburg is well-known. However, although Luther insisted on the presence in the elements, and the importance of the words, he showed no interest in setting out his doctrine of presence in systematic detail, which suggests that his interest in the words in the liturgical rite were for other reasons.

In *FM* Luther accepted the mass as a sacrament, eucharist, Lord's Supper, Lord's memorial, or communion, or any pious name except 'sacrifice'. But, as we have seen, his own preference was 'Testament'. It was a testament or promise of God's forgiveness, the promise of the sufficiency of the sacrifice on the cross for all men. He wrote:

'According to its substance, therefore, the mass is nothing but the aforesaid words of Christ: "Take and eat, etc", as if he were saying: "Behold, O sinful and condemned man, out of the pure and unmerited love with which I love you, and by the will of the Father of mercies, apart from any merit or desire of yours, I promise you in these words the forgiveness of all your sins and life everlasting. And that you may be absolutely certain of this irrevocable promise of mine, I shall give my body and pour out my blood, confirming this promise by my very death, and leaving you my body and blood as a sign and memorial of this same promise. As often as you partake of them, remember me, proclaim and praise my love and bounty toward you, and give thanks".'[5]

Elsewhere Luther claimed that these words constitute the mass; Christians must

'grasp and thoroughly ponder the words of Christ by which he performed and instituted the mass and command us to perform it. For therein lies the whole mass, its nature, work, profit, and benefit. Without the words nothing is derived from the mass.'[6]

---

[1] See also *Thomas Becon, op. cit.,* p.269, and John Knox, *A Vindication of the Doctrine that the Sacrifice of the Mass is Idolatry,* 1550, in *The Works of John Knox,* Ed. D. Laing, (6 vols., Edinburgh 1864), Vol. 3, pp.33-70, p.50. However, as Ratcliff has demonstrated, *'enim' is* found in the Old Latin version of Matthew, and was therefore scriptural! Elsewhere Luther seems to have approved its use. (*LW* 40.73).

[2] *LW* 36.277.   [3] *LW* 36.32.   [4] Brilioth, *op. cit.,* p.106.

[5] *LW* 36.40. cf. *LW* 35.85.[6] *LW* 35.82.

The reason was that the words of institution were in fact the gospel in a nutshell; they are a summary of the promise of the gospel:

> 'For if you ask: What is the gospel? you can give no better answer than these words of the New Testament, namely, that Christ gave his body and poured out his blood for the forgiveness of sins. . . . Therefore, these words, as a short summary of the whole gospel, are to be taught and instilled into every Christian's heart, . . .'[1]

> '. . . they are the sum and substance of the whole gospel.'[2]

If, then, these words are the gospel (i.e. justification) in a nutshell, then they must be proclaimed. Instead of a silent recitation, the words were to be intoned. In *FM* Luther suggested that they might be intoned to the same intonation as the Lord's Prayer, but evangelical freedom meant that they could still be recited silently. However, this freedom was withdrawn in *DM*. The gospel must be proclaimed, and the words of institution were to be chanted to the Gospel intonation. The chanting of the words, and to the Gospel tone, in *DM,* represents the logic of Luther's ideas on the Gospel and music. For Luther (cf. Barth on Mozart!) music was a beautiful and glorious gift of God; and God has preached the gospel through music too.[3] Music could usefully assist the proclamation of the gospel. Thus the sixth mode which was used for the chanting of the Gospel was used for the proclamation of the summary of the gospel. Paull Nettl writes of Luther's setting in *DM*:

> 'As with other texts which deeply stirred him, this too begins with a high note, "C", stressing the first syllable, *Unser.* Then the voice, as though in humility, drops a third and plays around with "A", then to sink down to the "F" at the second syllable of the word *Verraten,* as though expressing deep despair at the misdeeds of His disciple. There, where Jesus himself speaks, *Nempt,* the melody starts in with a low "F" with concise simplicity, moves around this repercussion tone, to rise at the phrase, *fur euch,* as if to give melodious expression to salvation by the Saviour's death. What we experience in this simple sequence of tones, full of symbolism, is tht deeply personal, sorrowful, yet consoling devotion which radiates from the mystery of the communion as Luther felt it.'[4]

As far as Luther was concerned, in emphasizing the words of institution, he was replacing the canon with the gospel itself, and in the gospel it is God who does something for us, and offers it to us. Here, then, is not a remnant of the canon prayed to God, but the gospel offering Christ and his forgiveness to us.

. . . C. The Elevation and the Sanctus

In the light of medieval emphasis on the elevation as the 'high point' in the mass and on its connection with transubstantiation, together with the fact that it was immediately abolished by most Reformers, Luther's retention of the elevation may seem an anachronism. But his writings suggest that he 'demythologized' it, and put it to a new use.

---

[1] *LW* 36.183. [2] *LW* 36.277.

[3] *LW* 54.129; Paul Nettl, *Luther and Music* (Muhlenberg Press, Philadelphia, 1948).

[4] Nettl, *op. cit.,* p.79.

Luther was fully aware of the dangers of the elevation. In *The Misuse of the Mass* he argued that it was the elevation that had influenced his opponents to call the mass a sacrifice. It would make no difference to the service if it was omitted because it was a human invention.[1] In the *Babylonian Captivity,* he had explained it as either a survival of a Hebrew rite of lifting up what was received with thanksgiving and returning it to God, or else an admonition to provoke faith in the Testament.[2] His suspicion of its possible implications is evident in *FM* where the reason for its retention is chiefly on account of the 'infirm' who might be greatly offended by a sudden change in the rite.

However, Luther also saw the elevation as a positive feature giving visual expression to the Testament in the words of institution. In his *Treatise on the New Testament,* he wrote:

'And this is what is meant when the priest elevates the host, by which he addresses us rather than God. it is as if he were saying to us, "Behold, this is the seal and the sign of the testament in which Christ has bequeathed to us the remission of all sins and eternal life". In agreement with this is also that which is sung by the choir, "Blessed be he who comes in the name of God", whereby we testify how (in the sacrament) we receive blessings from God, and do not sacrifice or give to God.'[3]

In *The Misuse of the Mass* he noted its positive nature:

'It may well signify, however, that just as this pledge of the promise of Christ is elevated in order that the people may thereby be inspired to faith, so the Word should be preached publicly to the people in order that everyone may hear the testament and see the pledge, and through both be attracted and aroused to faith and strengthened in it.'[4]

And it is this positive side of the elevation which was put forward in *DM*—it signifies that Christ has commanded us to remember him, and we may apprehend by faith how Christ gives us his body and blood. It is in fact a showing forth of the pledge of God's forgiveness. Bard Thompson has very aptly described it as a pictorial anamnesis.[5]

In *DM* Luther remarked that the elevation went well with the German *Sanctus.* In *FM* he had placed this anthem and the Benedictus qui venit after the words of institution, and in *DM* the Latin version was replaced by a German paraphrase. It will be recalled that Brilioth regarded this as 'without doubt one of the least successful of Luther's suggestions for reform'.[6] It would seem that Brilioth had paid more attention to comparative liturgy than to Luther.

To begin with, as we have already noted, at this time the Sanctus was simply regarded as an anthem before the canon, and not as part of it. There was, therefore, no reason why it should have been placed within a reformed canon. Luther did utilize it, however, as an anthem sung as a conclusion to his new canon. The reason for this new position seems to be two-fold. It came at the end of the words of institution during the elevation as a joyful response to the proclamation of the gospel, the testament of forgiveness; it was a thanksgiving—the sacrifice of praise

---

[1] *LW* 36.183. [2] *LW* 36.53. al [3] *LW* 35.87. [4] *LW* 36.183.
[5] Thompson, *op. cit.,* p.104. [6] Brilioth, *op. cit.,* p.117.

which follows the proclamation of justification. But there is a second reason which is not immediately apparent.

The Sanctus is taken from Isaiah 6.3, though a different version is found in Revelation 4.8. In the former, Isaiah is in the temple of Jerusalem before the presence of Yahweh; in the latter, the twenty-four elders in the heavenly city hear the four living creatures singing the Sanctus. Since in the eucharist the Sanctus followed the Sursum corda, it may be assumed that the worshipper lifted his heart and mind to join the Sanctus of the heavenly temple. Luther's German paraphrase shows that he preferred to see it as the Sanctus of Isaiah. Probably this is because he saw a distinct parallel in Isaiah 6 with the eucharist. In Isaiah 6 the prophet heard the Sanctus sung in honour of the holiness of God. Commenting on these verses Luther said:

> 'The angels were borne aloft like birds, that is, they served God not with their endeavours, but with a confession in which they sing the Trishagion, that is, the thrice holy, whereby they indicate that all holiness in the whole earth must be ascribed to God alone. All the words are grandly put. They shouted. The truest worship of God is a pure and simple confession. God says (Ps. 50.23): "He who brings thanksgiving as his sacrifice honours me". The other things we have, such as gifts, intellect, good habits, our best endeavours, let these be concealed. We must glory in the Word alone and confess that we have received these gifts from God, we do not bring them along. . . . It is necessary that God be hallowed and that I be defiled, but in that act of hallowing I must know, believe, praise, and confess that God Himself is alone holy, that He gives and does not receive.[1]

Luther saw the Sanctus as a true sacrifice of praise—something which men could render to God. But there is a deeper significance. Isaiah was overawed by a sense of sin. One of the seraphim cleansed him by putting a burning coal on his lips and saying, 'Behold, this has touched your lips; your guilt is taken away, and your sin forgiven'. Then the prophet was sent out as the servant of God. For Luther, the gospel and the mass were for sinners because both were a declaration of sins forgiven. The bread and wine are the tokens or seals of that promise, and they touch the lips of the communicant as a declaration of forgiveness. After communion, the Christian is sent out as a servant of God. Thus, the Sanctus fits the Testament of forgiveness.

In *DM* Luther suggested that the Sanctus might be sung during the distribution of the bread, before the words concerning the cup were proclaimed, and suggested specific hymns which could be sung in addition to the Sanctus. At the distribution of the wine, these hymns and the Agnus Dei could be sung. The two hymns and the Agnus Dei express that Christ has taken away the sin of the communicant.

Concluding Remarks on Luther's Canon
Having considered Luther's views on the canon and the constituent parts of his new Reformed canon, we conclude:

1. Luther's reformed canon, found in two forms, that of *FM* and *DM*, reaches its polished form in *DM*. It is sometimes asserted that Luther

[1] *LW* 16.70.

preferred *FM*. If this is applied to the form of the canon, it is difficult to explain why Luther made new recommendations. In part he saw that a German mass needed a different idiom, and needed to be more than a wooden translation from the Latin. However, it would seem that *DM* was also an opportunity to make clearer his intentions. *DM* itself explains why Luther still wanted *FM* to remain in use. He emphasized again and again the importance of retaining Latin in Bible lessons and services, because it helped the youth to learn Latin. The Latin liturgies were thus useful educationally. *FM* was important because it was in Latin, not because it had a 'better' canon.

2. Luther's new canon was *not* a remnant of the old. Such an idea arises by simply comparing the new canon with the old one. But clearly, any such comparison must take into account that between the old and the new stands Luther himself. Luther was adamant that the canon of the mass *must be removed in its entirety*. The fact that the words of institution occur in both may be regarded as a coincidence— the narrative was the sole saving grace of the old canon, but even here the words were not scriptural enough, and the words were addressed to God in prayer. In Luther the words are a proclamation of the gospel. *The reformed canon, then, is a deliberate new composition.*

3. The reason for the new canon is to be found in Luther's doctrine of justification by faith and its relation to the command 'Do this in remembrance of me'. The old canon was in obedience to this command, for throughout it spoke in terms of 'We do'. It was a response to God's action in Christ, seeking by faithful obedience and repetition and intercession, to enter into the sacrifice of Christ. This seems to have been precisely Luther's objection. For Luther, the sacrifice of the cross and forgiveness of sins were God's gift to man which could only be received with thanksgiving. It could not be actively entered into by man, whether by imitation or by intercession. 'Do this in remembrance of me' was to proclaim again what God had done for man, and Luther seems to have concluded that the most effective way of doing this was by letting God himself speak in the words of institution. Thus Luther's reformed canon replaced 'We do' with 'He has done'. His starting point was 'Dominus Dixit'. As he explained:

'"He sent forth his word, and thus (*sic*) healed them", not: "He accepted our work, and thus healed us".'[1]

Instead of trying to participate and enter into the sacrifice of Christ by lifting our hearts to the heavenly altar, we stand in awe with Isaiah as Christ speaks to us on earth, granting us pardon, and therefore taking us up into his sacrifice.[2] In doing this, Luther believed that he had replaced the canon with the gospel; the canon had given up its place at the marriage feast to Christ its master.

4. If this explanation of Luther is correct, then words such as 'conservative', and 'pruning-knife' or 'hatchet job', are completely inadequate, and even misleading. Far from being a conservative and unimaginative liturgiologist, Luther was in fact giving radical liturgical expression to justification by faith, and deserves to be regarded as a serious Reformation liturgist.

[1] *LW* 36.39. '*Sic*' is Luther's own interpolation into the Vulgate text.
[2] *LW* 35.99.

4. LUTHER AND THE EUCHARISTIC PRAYER TODAY

The purpose of this study has been to investigate Luther's reform of the canon by means of the Reformer's own premises rather than from the standpoint of earlier eucharistic prayers. As Hermann Sasse stresses, 'He must be understood from his own presuppositions. . . . If we want Luther to speak to us, we must allow him to speak in his language and on his terms even at the risk of hearing unexpected things. It may be that the unexpected . . . are more helpful . . .'[1]

However, the study does not necessarily assume that all Luther's presuppositions were correct, and it is not intended to imply that Luther's sixteenth century reform of the canon is a paradigm for modern anaphoral composition. Rather, in recent years many Lutheran Churches—in Germany, Sweden, and America—have either adopted or advocated eucharistic prayers which have been based on the pattern of the classical anaphoras.[2] Such eucharistic prayers have been criticized as both un-Lutheran, and, therefore, un-evangelical.

Eucharistic Prayers as Un-Lutheran—Three American Authors
A. In a series of articles, Oliver Olson sharply attacked the Inter-Lutheran Commission on Worship's *Contemporary Worship II* (1970).[3] as having accepted the views set forth by Odo Casel and Gregory Dix—particularly on the meaning of *anamnesis*—mediated to the Lutheran tradition by Peter Brunner.[4] Olson argued that Luther objected not just to the canon of the mass, but to *any* eucharistic prayer which might precede communion. In his view, euthentic Lutheran theology emphasizes the element of *newness* in the New Covenant, and the authority of Christ against that of the Old Testament and Jewish custom.[5] For Luther, 'This do' did not refer to the whole supper, and it did not even include the Jewish meal *berakoth* which recent liturgists have insisted underlies the eucharistic prayer.[6] The command referred not to Jewish traditions, but to the *newness* of his action, which was the act of eating and drinking the bread and wine which he had declared to be his body and blood.[7] Olson appealed to Jeremias's suggestion that the classical anaphoras are the result of a clumsy development based on confusion about the original function of the prayer, culminating in the words being inserted into the prayer and addressed to God instead of being separate and being proclaimed to the congregation.[8] In advocating a eucharistic prayer, the *ILCW* had dropped Luther's idea of 'Testament' and had substituted for it the Melanchthon-Zwingli idea of covenant requiring a response from men.[9]

[1] Hermann Sasse 'Luther and the Word of God' in (ed.) Kadai, *op. cit.,* p.50.
[2] Details in Joop Bergsma, 'The Eucharistic Prayer in the Non-Roman Catholic Churches of the West Today' in *SL* 11(1976), pp.177-185.
[3] Oliver K. Olson, 'Luther's Catholic Minimum' in *Response* 11 (1970), pp.17-31; 'Contemporary Trends in Liturgy viewed from the Perspective of Classical Lutheran Theology' in *Lutheran Quarterly* 26 (1974), pp.110-157; 'Liturgy as "Action" ' in *Dialog* 14(1975), pp.108-113.
[4] Peter Brunner *Worship in the Name of Jesus* (ET), Concordia, St. Louis, 1968).
[5] 'Luther's Catholic Minimum', p.9.
[6] For the *berakah* background, C. J. Cuming, *He Gave Thanks: An Introduction to the Eucharistic Prayer* (Grove Liturgical Study 28, Grove Books, Bramcote, 1981).
[7] 'Luther's Catholic Minimum', p.22.
[8] *Ibid.,* p.26.   [9] 'Contemporary Trends', p.152.

'Why not learn from the Presbyterians . . .? We could place a firm Amen after the first part of the eucharistic prayer, then direct the words of institution to the congregation, and then—after doing our homework on the *epiclesis* and *anamnesis* and deciding if such dubious practices can be understood in some evangelical way—we could continue praying.'[2]

B. Paul Rorem also has argued that Luther was opposed to the words of institution being within a prayer. So:

'A prayer could survey salvation history in praise and thanksgiving to God (as the Jewish *berakah*), while the Words of Institution would remain independently proclaimed to the worshippers as words which promise blessing and interpret the bread and wine (as the *haggadah*),'[2]

C. Gottried G. Krodel attacked *The Great Thanksgiving* (1975) of the *ILCW* as having abandoned Luther and the Lutheran *Confessions.* He rightly questions the widespread assumption that at the Last Supper Jesus used the *Birkat ha-mazon.* Like Olson and Rorem, Krodel insists that the institution should be a proclamation of the word, and not merely a narrative, whether addressed to God or man:

'If one has lost the quality of this Word—majestically and yet childlike and therefore beautifully expressed in Ps. 33.9—then, of course, one must introduce an Epiclesis . . .'[3]

Krodel suggests that 'remembrance' for Luther was understood in a *rhetorical* way, possibly being derived from Quintilian's *Institutio Oratoria,* a book introduced in Wittenberg University during the reforms of 1517—18. Quintilian sees a movement from facts, or ideas, to *memoria,* which faithfully stores the given facts or ideas; this is for him the process of remembering. *Memoria* or remembrance stands, then, in the middle between the given and the delivery; it need not lead to delivery, but delivery without *memoria* is impossible, as is a *memoria* without givens.[1]

For Luther, the bread and wine are a memorial *given* to us. 'Do this' refers to the eating and drinking of this specially designated bread and cup given to the disciples. Remembrance has to do with ceremonial remembering, proclaiming, and eating and drinking, *not* thanksgiving. Thus Krodel asserts:

'Luther sharply distinguishes between the testament—the Bread and Cup words—and whatever prayers surround these central words. He would reject any Lord's Supper liturgy that presents itself as "one continuous prayer—proclamation" or a liturgy in which the words are in a tail end, appendix position, or a liturgy in which there is absolutely no proclamation in the New Testament sense of the word, but only a freely composed "narrative".'[4]

Krodel stresses that for Luther the proper sequence after the proclamation of the Word is, receiving the Testament, and then offering

---

[1] 'Luther's Catholic Minimum', p.30.

[2] Paul Rorem, 'Luther's Objections to a Eucharistic Prayer' in *The Cresset* 38.5(1975), p.16—see pp.12-16 for the whole argument.

[3] Gottfried G. Krodel 'The Great Thanksgiving of the Inter-Lutheran Commission on Worship: It is the Christians' Supper and not the Lord's Supper' in *The Cresset* Occasional Paper 1, 1976—quotation from p.15.

[4] *Ibid.,* p.25.

our thanksgiving and praise.[1] He thus seems to advocate a refined version of *DM,* the 'eucharistic prayer' being a post-communion prayer.

A Swedish Solution?

Frank C. Senn has, in a recent article in *Studia Liturgica,* put forward the Swedish Lutheran canon in the 1576 'Red Book' of King Johan III as a model which expresses Lutheran theological convictions within the traditional form of a eucharistic prayer.[2] However at the time of its publication and ever since, this particular liturgy has been regarded as an unrepresentative aberration. As it contains the institution narrative, it is also open to the same criticisms as the modern eucharistic prayers.

Exegetical and Theological Clarification

A reading of the criticisms of Olson, Rorem and Krodel suggests that with considerable ease they have found the Achilles' heel of much modern liturgical revision and study: a preoccupation with historical liturgy of the fifth and sixth centuries, and certain liturgical dogmas, accepted as fact, but which rest upon highly tendentious arguments. Furthermore, all too often modern liturgists appear to function quite independently of and without reference to other theological disciplines, particularly biblical and systematic theology. Yet at the same time, these articles are disconcerting to non-Lutherans in the manner in which Luther's works are elevated almost to the status of *verba dei.* Reformation fundamentalism, while no worse, is certainly no better, than patristic fundamentalism. The irony is that Luther's liturgical work, or his principles, should suggest that liturgy should be on a firm theological base, and so it requires us not to retreat behind Luther's words and his reforms, but to engage with biblical and systematic theology. The institution is a good example.

(1) New Covenant. Luther seems to have preferred the word 'testament' to 'covenant'. However, although he borrowed the terminology from Chrysostom, he developed it in the context of the Epistle to the Hebrews—ironically a work which in 1522 he assigned to a lesser canonical position. He expounded the *diatheke* of the Lord's Supper from the standpoint of Hebrews. But it must be asked whether a wider understanding of covenant in the Bible is a more helpful and legitimate aproach to its meaning in the institution? The Mesopotamian vassal treaty which may underlie many of the Old Testament references to covenant was certainly not an agreement between equals.[3] A celebration of the New Covenant may well require a *haggadah,* but does this automatically exclude a eucharistic prayer before com-munion? While the present state of research on the eucharistic prayer suggests that, unlike *Apostolic Tradition,* the early eucharistic prayer in Egypt and East Syria did not contain the institution narrative—thus upholding Lutheran objections—, we cannot be certain that those rites included no institution narrative *at all.* It was precisely because of the New Covenant *haggadah*—which is the eternal word of God—that the church assembled to 'Do this'. Was this eternal proclamation taken for granted? In obedience and faith, can the Church assemble to celebrate the memorial until he comes *without reciting the narrative at all?*

[1] *Ibid.,* p.23.
[2] Frank C. Senn 'Liturgia Svecanae Ecclesiae: An Attempt at Eucharistic Restoration during the Swedish Reformation' in *SL* 14(1980-81), pp.20-36.
[3] D. J. McCarthy *Old Testament Covenant: A Survey of Current Opinions* (O.U.P., 1972).